Early Indian Campaigns and the Decorations Awarded for them.

BY
MAJOR H. BIDDULPH, R.E.

❖

The Naval & Military Press Ltd

❖

Published by

The Naval & Military Press Ltd

Unit 10, Ridgewood Industrial Park,

Uckfield, East Sussex,

TN22 5QE England

Tel: +44 (0) 1825 749494

Fax: +44 (0) 1825 765701

www.naval–military–press.com

EARLY INDIAN CAMPAIGNS AND THE DECORATIONS AWARDED FOR THEM.

INTRODUCTION.

WHEN my interest in medals was first awakened, I found that there was no book in existence which gave accurate information as to the troops engaged in the old Indian Campaigns for which medals were granted. Some books indeed there were which treated of the subject, but they were so incomplete and inaccurate as to be of little value. This is probably due to the fact that information as to the Native corps engaged in battles fought so long ago is not very accessible ; while the renumbering of the Indian armies in 1824, followed by the Mutiny in 1857, which swept away most of the Bengal Army and led to the renumbering once more of the corps which survived, complicated the matter still further.

Having unusual facilities for obtaining correct information on this subject, as also on the issue, etc., of the medals in question, I compiled for my own use a number of notes ; which I have now recast for the benefit of collectors. A certain amount of very interesting information I have felt compelled to withhold ; for it is not my wish to facilitate the faker's task ; his sphere of labours is already too extensive.

The period covered by these notes is 50 years, 1799—1849. The medals, issued by the H.E.I.C. to its Native troops only, have not been dealt with in detail. To have included the Indian Mutiny would have almost doubled the size of the book ; the number of medals issued for that campaign was enormous ; the vast majority being without a clasp or issued to Native or irregular and local corps of every sort.

It is not generally known however that at least 49 Europeans and 79 Natives earned the Mutiny medal with four clasps.

To make the subject complete descriptions and illustrations of the different medals have been included, and a very brief narrative of each campaign is also given. The various lists of Engineer officers have been inserted as a tribute to the Corps to which I belong.

H. BIDDULPH.

A 2

MYSORE, 1780–99.

No less than three wars were waged by the H.E.I.C.S. against Hyder Ali and his son Tippoo Sahib, successive rulers of Mysore. The first war, 1780–4, is notable for the defeat of Colonel Baillie, the defence of Wandewash and the Siege of Cuddalore, when the original 24th Bengal Native Infantry defeated the French European troops at the bayonet's point, taking prisoner the Chevalier de Damas and Sergeant Bernadotte, better known in later years as the King of Sweden.

The second war 1790–2 was undertaken by Lord Cornwallis in person, as the opening phase of the campaign was mismanaged by the local commander-in-chief. Bangalore was stormed and taken on the night of 21st March, 1791, and the army advanced on Seringapatam, defeating Tippoo at Arikera, a few miles from his capital. At the end of May just before the arrival of the force co-operating from the Bombay side under Major-General Robert Abercromby, Lord Cornwallis ordered a retreat on account of the abnormal rains, and the consequent loss of transport and failure of supplies. In the ensuing cold weather Cornwallis marched once more on Seringapatam and on the 6/7th February was fought the great battle on the island, which ended finally in the complete defeat of Tippoo, who lost 76 guns and some 20,000 men. Among the killed was Lieut. Patrick Stewart, Bengal Engineers. Tippoo then sued for peace, which was granted on his agreeing to cede an enormous tract of his territory and the payment of a war indemnity of 33 million rupees (about £4,000,000 stg.).

For both these wars the H.E.I.C. granted medals, but to the *native* ranks only; the native officers receiving medals in gold or silver according to their rank, while native non-commissioned officers and men received similar silver medals of smaller size.

The third Mysore war was undertaken in 1799, the chief command being vested in Lieut.-General George Harris, while a force under Lieut.-General Jas. Stuart co-operated from the Bombay side. This campaign is notable as being the second occasion on which the future Duke of Wellington, then Colonel the Hon. A. Wellesley saw service in the field. He commanded the Nizam's detachment to which his regiment, the 33rd Foot, was attached. The Madras and Bombay columns met with little opposition and concentrated beneath the walls of Seringapatam early in April, 1799.

The siege was commenced. On the 4th May the breach was stormed at midday, and Tippoo fell in the assault.

No less than 934 guns, howitzers and mortars were captured with the fortress; and the prize money amounted to £1,143,216, probably a record for British troops. A special medal was granted by the Company to *all* ranks; general officers receiving it in gold, field officers in silver-gilt, other European officers in silver, British sergeants and drummers in copper-bronzed, as also Native officers, havildars and drummers of the Madras and Bombay Armies, while inferior ranks received it in grain tin.

The die was copied in Calcutta and the Bengal Government following their usual practice, issued gold medals to the native officers, and silver medals to other native ranks of the Bengal native troops present at the siege.

A detailed list of the troops engaged is appended, together with a description of the medals issued and notes thereon. It was not until 1851 that the *Queen's* troops received official sanction to wear this medal on all occasions.

SERINGAPATAM, 1799.

(*a*). English Die ; 1·9 in. diameter.
  Gold, silver-gilt, silver, copper-bronzed, tin.
(*b*). Calcutta Die ; 1·8 in. diameter.
  Gold, silver.

Obverse.—A tiger struck down by a lion ; inscription in Arabic "The conquering Lion of God." "iv. May, MDCCXCIX."
Reverse.—The storming of the breach at midday.
    Persian inscription in exergue "The God-granted Fortress of Seringapatam, 4th May, 1799."
Ribbon.—Watered yellow, or crimson with blue edges, 1¾ in. wide.

N.B.—The inscriptions on the medal have a double meaning : "The conquering Tiger (Lion) of God" was one of Tippoo's attributes ; but in this instance is applied to the British Lion instead of to Tippoo's Tiger ; while the phrase "The God-granted Fortress of Seringapatam" which here signifies the conquest of it by the British, signified previously to Tippoo's subjects that his sovereignty over Seringapatam was of Divine origin, both phrases being customary ones of Tippoo's.

The Medal for the Capture of Seringapatam, 1799, *etc.*

Much difference of opinion has prevailed as to the ribbon actually worn with the Seringapatam medal. That it was intended to be orange-coloured admits of no doubt, the statement on this point of General Sir J. L. Caldwell, Madras Engineers, (who received the medal) cannot be traversed. As, however, no ribbon was issued with the medal, everybody entitled to wear it had to provide it for themselves, and it is certain that a very large number of officers wore it suspended from the broad crimson and blue ribbon worn with Peninsula gold medals, which was the "military" ribbon of Great Britain. Examination of portraits, engravings, etc., show that Lord Harris, Sir David Baird, Sir Thos. Munro, Lord Combermere and others wore it in this way, some round the neck and others at the button hole ; and it has been denied that the orange ribbon was worn by anybody.   This, however, can be disproved, portraits of Sir John Malcolm and of Sir Robert Sale show distinctly the orange ribbon.   Sir John Malcolm, who served as a captain at the siege in command of the Nizam's contingent, died in 1833, his portrait shows him wearing the gold or silver-gilt medal with an orange ribbon.   Sir R. Sale served as a subaltern in the 12th Foot at Seringapatam, and his portrait as a Major-General appears to have been taken when he was at home on leave in 1844, after the close of the Afghan War.   He is depicted wearing the Seringapatam medal with orange ribbon, the Ghuznee, Cabul and 2nd Jellalabad medals. The addition by the recipient of a heavy clasp, in gold or silver, inscribed " Seringapatam," was not uncommon in the case of officers.

With regard to the issue of the medal, it is to be noted that it was given not only as a war medal to the troops engaged at the siege or in the neighbourhood, but also as a commemorative medal to various personages and officials of high rank, and also to at least one military officer who was not present, viz. :—Major-General John Braithwaite, Adjutant-General, Madras Presidency.   This fact detracts considerably from the interest attaching to all medals issued by the H.E.I.C. for various services ranging from 1778—1826, as one can very rarely be certain that any individual medal was actually worn by a soldier, and still less often as to who (if any) the wearer was.   Re-strikes also, of all these medals, except that for Ava, are not uncommon. The dies of the Ava medal are at the Royal Mint, and re-strikes do not exist except the few issued as specimens with representative sets of medals ; but original silver proofs perhaps exist.   The dies of the Seringapatam medal, English die, are in private hands, and those of other medals at the Calcutta Mint ; as it is only within the last few years that the Calcutta Mint has been prohibited from issuing re-strikes, they are by no means uncommon.

The Egypt (1801), Java and Nepaul dies are now cracked, and specimens showing these flaws are sometimes seen.

The dies of the 1784 Carnatic medal (commonly but erroneously called the Deccan medal), and of the Mysore medal, 1791–2, are not in existence ; but castings are met with.

Medals from the Calcutta-made Seringapatam dies were struck in gold and silver for the Natives of the Bengal troops that served at the siege, Native officers receiving the gold medal, and other ranks the medal in silver.   The Bengal troops present consisted of four companies of Bengal Foot Artillery and eight companies of Lascars, the 1st and 2nd Battalions of the 10th Bengal Infantry, and the 1st, 2nd and 3rd Volunteer Battalions from Bengal ; after the war the 18th and 19th Regiments of Bengal N. Infantry (each of two battalions) were formed from these three Volunteer battalions.

The Seringapatam medal was the only one of this series that was issued to Europeans, with the exception of one gold medal presented to Sir Archibald Campbell, Commander-in-Chief of the expedition to Ava, 1824–26, and for this reason it has been discussed somewhat fully.

Troops engaged at

(1). *Siege and Capture of Seringapatam*, 1799.

Commander-in-Chief :—Lieut.-General G. Harris.

Madras Troops.

Cavalry :—Major-General J. Floyd, 19th Light Dragoons.

1st Brigade :—*Colonel J. Stevenson, 4th Madras Cavalry.
H.M. 19th Light Dragoons (430 men).
1st and 4th Madras Cavalry.

2nd Brigade :—*Colonel J. Pater, 2nd Madras Cavalry.
H.M. 25th Light Dragoons (454 men).
2nd and 3rd Madras Cavalry.

Guides :—Major J. Campbell.

Artillery :—Major-General D. Smith, Madras Artillery.
1st and 2nd Battns. Madras Artillery.

1 Co. Coast Artillery (serving with Nizam's detachment).
†3-1st, ‡5-2nd, 1-3rd and 2-3rd Battns. Bengal Artillery,
and 8 Companies Lascars.

Engineers :—Colonel W. Gent, Madras Engineers.

Corps of Pioneers.

Infantry :—Right Wing:—Major-General T. Bridges, 1st Madras N.I.
1st Brigade :—Major-General D. Baird.
H.M. 12th Foot (693 men).
„ 74th Foot (789 „).
„ Scotch Brigade (559).

3rd Brigade :—Colonel F. Gowdie, Madras N.I.
1-6th, 1-12th and 1-1st Madras N.I.

5th Brigade :—Colonel G. Roberts, Madras N.I.
2-3rd, 1-8th and 2-12th Madras N.I.

Left Wing :—Major-General W. Popham, 7th Bengal N.I.
2nd Brigade :—Colonel J. C. Sherbrooke, 33rd Foot.
H.M. 73rd Foot (746 men).
§Swiss Regiment de Meuron (715 men).

---

* Both these officers entered the H.E.I.C.S. from that of the Nawab of Arcot as Captains in 1784. They both attained General Officer's rank. Stevenson served with Wellesley in 1803–4.

† The 3-1st Bengal Artillery served with the Nizam's detachment.

‡ The 5-2nd Bengal Artillery served with Colonel A. Brown's force; having recently come from Ceylon.

§ The Regiment de Meuron was originally in Ceylon in the pay of the Dutch. On the capture of that island by the British it accepted service under the Crown, and was removed to India.

4th Brigade :—Lieut.-Colonel J. Gardiner, 1-4th Bengal N.I.
*1st, 2nd and 3rd Volunteer Battalions from Bengal.
6th Brigade :—Lieut.-Colonel T. Scott, Scotch Brigade.
2-5th and 2-9th Madras N.I.

Nizam's Detachment :—

†Colonel the Hon. A. Wellesley, 33rd Foot.

H.M. 33rd Foot (879 men).

1st and 2nd Brigades :—Lieut.-Colonel J. Dalrymple, Madras N.I.
1st Brigade :—Lieut.-Colonel L. Grant, 10th Bengal N.I.
1-10th and 2-10th Bengal N.I.
2-11th Madras N.I.
2nd Brigade :—Lieut.-Colonel T. Bowser, Madras N.I.
2-2nd, 2-7th and 1-11th Madras N.I.
Artillery :—Major R. Howley, Madras Artillery.
3-1st Bengal Artillery.
1 Company Coast Artillery.
Lascars.
Nizam's Infantry (with guns) :—‡Capt. J. Malcolm, Madras N.I.
4 Battalions of Infantry (the old French contingent,
3,600 strong, to which two troops of disciplined
cavalry were attached).
Nizam's Cavalry :—Mir Alam. 6,000 strong.

Bombay Troops.

Commander-in-Chief :—Lieut.-General Jas. Stuart.

Artillery :—Lieut.-Colonel G. A. Lawman, Bombay Artillery.
3rd, 4th and 5th Companies.

Engineers and Pioneers :—Colonel J. C. Sartorius, Bombay Engineers.

Infantry :—§Major-General J. Hartley, 75th Foot.

Right Brigade :—Lieut.-Colonel J. Montresor, 77th Foot.
1-2nd, 1-4th and 1-3rd Bombay N.I.

Centre Brigade :—Lieut.-Colonel J. Dunlop, 77th Foot.
H.M. 75th Foot (223 men).
The Bombay European Regiment (528 men).
H.M. 77th Foot (693 men).

---

* The three Volunteer Battalions from Bengal were formed of volunteers from every regiment in Bengal except the 10th Regiment, Bengal N.I.
† Later 1st Duke of Wellington.
‡ Afterwards Sir J. Malcolm, G.C.B.
§ Hartley was transferred as a Lieut.-Colonel from the Bombay Army to the Lieut.-Colonelcy of H.M. 75th Foot, when that regiment was raised for service in India in 1787.

Left Brigade :—Lieut.-Colonel J. Wiseman, Bombay European
         Regiment.
        2-3rd, 1-5th and 2-2nd Bombay N.I.

(N.B.—The 2-3rd Bombay N.I. had detachments from other regiments).

On the 1st April, 1779, Major-General Floyd was detached with all the regular Cavalry and the 3rd Infantry Brigade (Gowdie) to meet a convoy under Colonel A. Read. Read met Floyd at Cowdahully at the end of April, was joined by Colonel Brown's detachment on the 6th May, and the whole force returned to Seringapatam with the convoy on the 11th May.

Colonel A. Read, 2-4th Madras N.I.

Capt. M. Cosby's Troop.
6 Troops Nizam's Horse.
Madras Artillery (36 men).
Nizam's   do.
1st Madras European Regiment (69 men).
Convalescents H.M. Foot (40 men).
Flankers 1-4th Madras N.I.
    do.   1-5th Madras N.I.
Battn. Companies 2-4th Madras N.I.
Nizam's Infantry.
Pioneers.
        In all 5,280 men.

Lieut.-Colonel A. Brown, Madras Infantry.

5-2nd Bengal Artillery (44 men).
Madras Artillery (55 men).
5 Companies H.M. 19th Foot (386 men).
Madras European Regiment (617 men).
Bengal Lascars.
Madras   do.
New Troops N. Cavalry.
3 Companies 2-1st M.N.I.
Battn. Companies 1-2nd M.N.I.
    ,,   ,,   1-3rd M.N.I.
Flankers 2nd and 3rd Regiments, M.N.I.
Flankers 13th Regiment, M.N.I.
Pioneers.
        In all 4,300 men.

Both these detachments shared in the prize money, the estimated total value of which was £1,143,216; and although not actually present at the siege it is probable that they were granted the medal also.

(2). *Assault of Seringapatam, 4th May,* 1799.

Major-General D. Baird in command of the assaulting column.

Right Column :—Colonel J. C. Sherbrooke.

    Flankers, Scotch Brigade.

     do. Regiment de Meuron.

    H.M. 73rd and 74th Regiments.

    Flankers, 2-2nd, 2-3rd, 1-11th and 2-12th Madras N.I.

     do. 1-2nd, 2-2nd, 1-3rd, 2-3rd, 1-4th, 1-5th

      Bombay N.I.

    50 Gunners and Lascars.

Forlorn Hope :—*Lieut. V. Hill, 74th Regiment, with 1 sergeant

    and 12 men, supported by 25 men.

Left Column :—Lieut.-Colonel J. Dunlop.

    Flankers, H.M. 75th, 77th and Bombay European

    Regiment.

    H.M. 12th and 33rd Regiments.

    Flankers, 1-10th, 2-10th Bengal N.I., and the 3 Volun-

    teer Battalions, Bengal N.I.

    50 Gunners and Lascars.

Forlorn Hope :—†Lieut. A. Lawrence, 77th Regiment, with 1

    sergeant and 12 men, supported by 25 men.

Half the corps of Pioneers accompanied each column.

The casualties during the siege were :—

Officers	...	22 killed.	45 wounded.		
Europeans	...	181 ,,	624 ,,	22 missing.	
Natives	...	119 ,,	420 ,,	100 ,,	

934 guns, howitzers and mortars were captured with the fortress.

ENGINEER OFFICERS WHO SERVED IN THE MYSORE WARS.

1ST MYSORE WAR, 1780–4.

Only Madras Engineers employed.

1780.—*With Colonel Baillie's Force.*

Capt. Jno. Theobald, killed at Perambankum, 10. 9. 80.

Ensign — Brunton, taken prisoner, and died in Seringapatam

1781–2.—*With Sir Eyre Coote's Army.*

Capt. Alex. Dugood, killed at Chittoor, 10. 11. 81.

 ,, Jas. Johnston, at Negapatam in 1782.

 ,, Wm. Gent.

Lieut. Jno. Wickens, to Negapatam 24. 9. 81, with Coote in 1782.

Ensign Rd. Baker.

 ,, Chas. Parsons Ogg.

 ,, Geo. Bong, sent to destroy Fort Pulicat, December, 1781.

    * Killed in the assault.

    † Father of Sir H. M. Lawrence.

1781–2.—With the Southern Army.
*Major Thos. Geils, Chief Engineer; at Siege of Negapatam and
    Trincomalee.
Lieut. Jno. Wickens, at Siege of Negapatam.
 „   Chas. Salmon, A.D.C. to Colonel Jno. Braithwaite, 13. 2. 82.

	Capt. Geo. Banks, to Trincomalee from Trichinopoli, 30. 7. 82.
Capitulation of Trincomalee, 30. 8. 82.	Ensign Rob. Watson, „ „ Negapatam, 30. 7. 82.
	„ Crawford Lennox, „ 30. 7. 82.

Ensign Wm. Collins Tyson, to Negapatam vice Watson, 30. 7. 82.

1783.—With Major-General Jas. Stuart's Army.
†Lieut.-Colonel Pat. Ross, Chief Engineer.
Capt. Jas. Johnston.
 „   Geo. Banks.
Lieut. Jno. Wickens, A.D.C. to Chief Engineer.
Ensign C. P. Ogg.
 „   Jacob Hemming.
 „   Dan. Jennings.
 „   Jno. Norris.
 „   Sam. Saunter.

1783.—With the Southern Army.
Capt. Jno. Byres or Bryres, from July, 1783, as Chief Engineer
Lieut. Chas. Salmon.

2ND MYSORE WAR, 1790–2.
Bengal Engineers.
S. Capt. Alex. Kyd, A.D.C. to Lord Cornwallis.
S. Lieut. Pat. Stewart, killed 6. 2. 92 at Seringapatam.
S. Ensign Jos. Stokoe, commanding Pioneers.
S. „   Jas. Tillyer Blunt.
S. Two other officers, names unknown.

Madras Engineers.
S. Lieut.-Colonel Pat. Ross, Chief Engineer.
B. Major Geo. Maule, Chief Engineer.
    Capt. Elisha Trapand, to Tanjore, G.O., 11. 5. 91.

* [Lieut. Thos. Geils, Madras Artillery, served with the Engineers from
1768–87, when he returned to the Artillery as Lieut.-Colonel and Commandant. A MS. *Army List* of 1787 shows him as Major of Engineers
and Lieut.-Colonel Commandant of Artillery, his name being entered in
the lists of both corps.]
† N.B.—When the Corps of Madras Engineers was put on a purely
military basis, and reorganized, 15th September, 1770, Capt.-Lieut. Pat.
Ross of the Royal Engineers was brought out from England as Chief
Engineer, with the rank of Lieut.-Colonel.

Capt. J. A. Kissellbeck, to Vizagapatam, G.O., 31. 8. 91 ; died 24. 5. 92.

B.   „   C. P. Ogg, to Ganjam, G.O., 31. 8. 91. To Trichinopoli, G.O., 15. 2. 92.

Lieut. Wm. Wynn Ryland ; sick 6. 11. 90 ; died 12. 6. 91.

       „   Geo. Bong.

S.   „   Jacob Hemming ; wounded 6/7th February, 1792.

S.   „   Mich. Russell, Adjutant, vice Cree, killed.

B.S.   „   Jno. Norris.

B.S.   „   Walter C. Lennon, commanding Pioneers.

B.S.   „   Colin Mackenzie, A.D.C. to Lieut.-Colonel P. Ross.

B. Ensign Alex. Cree, Adjutant, killed at Ryacottah, July, 1791.

       „   David Barclay, died at Trichinopoli, 9. 7. 90.

B.   „   Geo. Johnston, to Coimbatore, end of 1791.

B.S.   „   Thos. Wood, from September, 1790.

B.S.   „   Jas. L. Caldwell, twice wounded.

B.S.   „   Jno. W. Pyefinch.

S.   „   G. C. G. Pittman.

S.   „   Wm. Farquhar.

Bombay Engineers.

S. Major J. C. Sartorius, Chief Engineer with Major-General Robt. Abercromby.

S. Capt. Wm. H. Blackford, wounded.

Lieut. Fras. Stuart, killed at Dharwar, 14. 1. 91.

S. Ensign Jno. Johnson, with Little's detachment.

Three other officers, names unknown.

           B. *Signifies engaged in the Bangalore Campaign.*

           S.   „   „   *Seringapatam Campaign.*

3RD MYSORE WAR, 1799.

Madras Engineers.

Colonel Wm. Gent, Chief Engineer.

Major Elisha Trapaud.

Capt. Jno. Norris, A.D.C. to Chief Engineer.

    „   Colin Mackenzie, Chief Engineer, Nizam's detachment.

    „   Geo. Johnston.

Capt.-Lieut. Jas. L. Caldwell, twice wounded.

       „   Jno. Blair.

Lieut. Wm. Castle.

    „   Thos. Fiott d'Havilland, with Brown's detachment.

    „   Jno. Cotgrave.

    „   Ben. Sydenham.

    „   Jno. Ross Cleghorn.

PLATE I.

EARLY INDIAN CAMPAIGNS AND THE DECORATIONS
AWARDED FOR THEM.

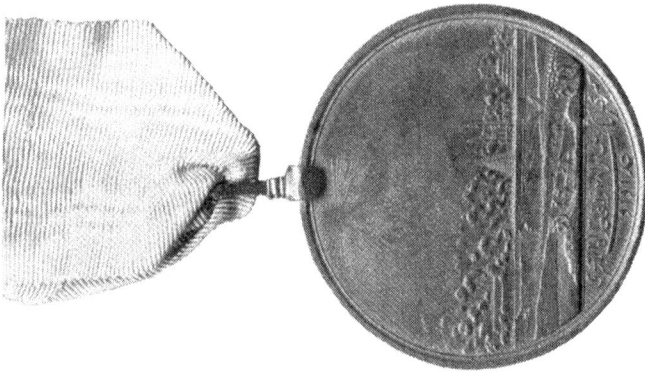

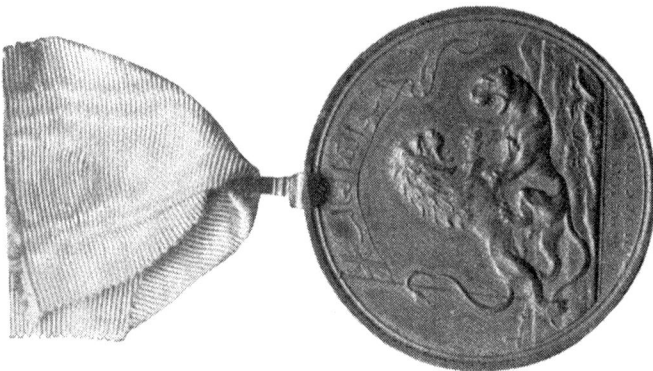

SERINGAPATAM. 1799.

Ensign Thos. Fraser, adjutant, wounded at Malavelly, 27. 3. 99, later with Read's detachment.

Thos. Arthur.

Wm. Gerrard.

Geo. Rowley.

Ensign Edw. Malton.

„ Chas. W. Bell.*

„ Jno. Smith.

Bombay Engineers.

Lieut.-Colonel J. C. Sartorius.

Ensign Jno. Johnson.

THE ARMY OF INDIA, 1803–26.

In 1847–8 the issue of a medal and clasps was authorized by the Queen to the survivors of the army who had served at those battles, sieges, etc., from 1806—1814, for which gold medals had been granted at the time to the general and commanding officers engaged. The only service included in this list in which troops from India had been engaged was the expedition to Java, 1811. Consequently, in 1851, a medal was authorized to those surviving soldiers, European and Native, who had served at certain battles, sieges, etc., in India from 1803—1826, as set forth below, with the following exceptions, viz. :—Such native soldiers as had received the medal for the Nepaul War, granted at the time by the H.E.I.C.S., were ineligible for the Queen's medal and clasp for this campaign ; and for the same reason no native was eligible for the Queen's medal and clasp for " Ava."

It will be noted that the date on the medal is 1799—1826, whereas the services for which it was granted were between 1803—1826. The reason for this discrepancy is that originally it was intended to include the Mysore War and Capture of Seringapatam in 1799 in the list of services for which the medal would be granted ; but it was pointed out that the H.E.I.C.S. had granted medals at the time to *all* ranks, both European and Native. This service therefore was struck out of the list, and authority given for troops in the service of the Crown to wear that medal on all occasions, but the date on the new medal die escaped observation.

Medal to the Army of India, 1799—1826. (1803–26). Authorized 1851.

1·4-in. diameter. Silver.

Obverse.—Crowned head of Queen Victoria.

Legend : " Victoria Regina."

Reverse.—Victory seated beside a palm tree and trophy.

Inscription : " To the Army of India, 1799—1826."

* [N.B.—Ensign C. W. Bell was transferred to the cavalry permanently on 28. 6. 01 and served with the 6th Madras Light Cavalry at Asseerghur, Argaum and Gawilghur in 1803.]

Ribbon.—Pale blue, 1¼ in. wide.

Mounting.—Silver scroll bar and swivel.

Clasps.—Allighur, Battle of Delhi, Laswaree, Defence of Delhi, Battle of Deig, Capture of Deig, Assye, Asseerghur, Argaum, Gawilghur, Nepaul, Kirkee, Poona, Kirkee and Poona, Corygaum, Seetabuldee, Nagpore, Seetabuldee and Nagpore, Maheidpoor, Ava, Bhurtpoor.

The medal rolls for the Europeans of the Queen's troops exist practically intact, though there is a strong suspicion that a few names may be missing. The reason of this is that claims came in piece-meal from 1851 to 1858, and the rolls were made up in batches, some of the later rolls containing a few names only. It is probable that some rolls containing a few names were mislaid before they were bound.

For the Europeans in the Company's service no proper medal roll exists; only a rough book of issues, which is almost certainly incomplete, although perhaps the entries omitted are few. The original rolls are probably in India. For the Native troops, such rolls as exist are to be found for the most part in India, and as (for the reasons stated above) they are to be numbered in dozens, were scattered over seven years, and emanated from different Presidencies, the verification of a Native's medal is more a matter of luck than anything else.

One thing, however, is certain, viz.; that practically every medal issued to a native, was sent out to India unengraved; and in that country some were rudely punched, others engraved, and probably a good number were issued plain.

Subject to the above remarks the following brief notes on the Army of India medal and the campaigns for which it was granted, may be of interest:—

Medal to the Army of India.

(i.). *Lake's Campaign*, 1803–4.

8th Light Dragoons	..	42 medals issued (officers & men)	
27th ,, ,,	..	20 ,, ,, ,, ,,	
29th ,, ,,	..	14 ,, ,, ,, ,,	
22nd Foot ..	..	8 ,, ,, ,, ,,	
76th Foot ..	..	31 ,, ,, ,, ,,	
H.E.I. Co.'s Service	..	52 ,, ,, *to Europeans* (officers & men)	

(ii.). *Wellesley's Campaign*, 1803.

19th Light Dragoons	..	13 medals issued (officers & men)	
74th Foot ..	..	20 ,, ,, ,, ,,	
78th Foot ..	..	37 ,, ,, ,, ,,	
94th Foot ..	..	40 ,, ,, ,, ,,	
H.E.I. Co.'s Service and miscellaneous ..	..	27 ,, ,, *to Europeans* (officers & men)	

(iii.). *"Kirkee and Poona."* Single bar.

65th Foot	16 medals issued (officers & men)	
H.E.I.C. Service (Europeans)	71 ,, ,, ,, ,,	

(iv.). *" Poona."* Single bar.

65th Foot	44 medals issued (officers & men)	
H.E.I.C. Service (*Europeans*)	32 ,, ,, ,, ,,	
" Poona," " Ava " ..	5 ,, ,, ,, ,,	
" Poona," " Bhurtpoor"..	1 ,, ,, ,, ,,	

(v.). *" Maheidpoor."* Single bar.

22nd Light Dragoons ..	28 medals issued (officers & men)	
1st Foot	12 ,, ,, ,, ,,	
H.E.I.C. Service and Miscellaneous (*Europeans*)	83 ,, ,, ,, ,,	

" Maheidpoor," " Ava."

1st Foot	19 ,, ,, ,, ,,	
H.E.I.C. Service (*Europeans*)	18 ,, ,, ,, ,,	

(vi.). *Nagpore.* Single bar.

1st Foot —	40 medals issued (officers & men)	
H.E.I.C. Service (*Europeans*)	43 ,, ,, ,, ,,	

" Nagpore," " Ava."

1st Foot	43 ,, ,, ,, ,,	
H.E.I.C. Service (*Europeans*)	5 ,, ,, ,, ,,	

(vii.). " *Nagpore*," " *Maheidpoor*," four medals issued to Europeans (officers and men).

" *Nagpore*," " *Maheidpoor*," " *Ava*," three medals issued to Europeans (officers and men).

" *Nepaul*," " *Maheidpoor*," one medal issued to European officer.

" *Nepaul*," " *Nagpore*," four medals issued to Europeans (officers and men).

" *Nagpore*," " *Bhurtpoor*," one medal issued to European officer.

(viii.). The *total* number of certain rare clasps, issued singly, and in combination with others, to Europeans and Natives, appears to be as follows :—

" *Seetabuldee and Nagpore*," 20 Europeans and 194 Natives.

" *Corygaum*." Single bar. 8 medals in all.

" *Poona*," " *Corygaum*," 10 medals in all.

" *Kirkee and Poona*," " *Corygaum*," 73 medals in all.

" *Asseerghur*," " *Kirkee and Poona*," " *Corygaum*," 1 medal.

The information about certain other rare clasps is somewhat indefinite, for it is not clear how many Natives received them. For instance, it is possible that a good many received the clasp " Kirkee " who were survivors of the 1st (Dapuri) Battalion, Peishwa's Brigade, Poona Auxiliary Force (afterwards the 23rd Bombay N.I.), which was engaged at the Battle of Kirkee, but not at the Battle of Poona, but the available records of any such issues are very indefinite. Only one man of the 65th Foot received the clasp " Kirkee," and this medal is in Lord Cheylesmore's collection. Another man of the 65th Foot received the two clasps " Poona," " Corygaum " ; this medal came into Dr. Payne's possession, but the " Corygaum " clasp was removed, owing to a most unfortunate misapprehension, and the medal has been irretrievably damaged.

I am not aware that there exists in any collection *genuine* specimens of medals with the clasps " Seetabuldee " or " Defence of Delhi " ; while to my certain knowledge several medals with fraudulent " Corygaum " bars have been sold in recent years, and fetched very high prices.

The numbers of medals issued for " Nepaul," " Ava " and " Bhurtpoor " are too numerous to require cataloguing. The number of naval recipients of the medal and clasp for " Ava " will be given later.

MAHRATTA WAR, 1803–5.

This war was occasioned by the jealousy of the Mahratta confederation at the expanding influence of the British power.

Scindia, Maharajah of Gwalior, and Bhoonsla, Rajah of Berar, were the two foes opposed to the British at the moment ; and the operations may be roughly divided into those conducted by General G. Lake, with the Grand Army, in the Doab, and those conducted by Major-General the Hon. A. Wellesley (and Colonel James Stevenson, commanding the Hydrabad Subsidiary Force), in the Deccan. Minor operations in Cuttack and Bundelkhund were undertaken by small detached forces.

Lake's Operations, 1803.

The Grand Army was directed to concentrate at Secundra on the 26th August, 1803,* and on the 27th (before the concentration was complete) Lake marched. On 29th August, an insignificant cavalry skirmish took place at Coel, before Allighur, which ended in the retreat of the Mahratta cavalry under Fleury, a Frenchman, who thereupon made a raid on Shekoabad, in British territory.

On the 3rd September Lake determined to seize by a *coup de main* the fort of Allighur, which was held by a garrison of several thousand men under the command of M. Pedron, son-in-law to M. Perron, Scindia's French Commander-in-Chief.

* For composition of force see later on.

The assaulting party was composed of four companies H.M.
76th Foot, supported by the 1-4th N.I. and four companies 2-17th
N.I., under the command of Brigadier the Hon. W. Monson, 76th
Foot. The surprise, which was timed for 4.30 a.m. failed, and the
assaulting party thereupon tried to escalade the walls ; a fruitless
attempt carried on for a long time under a heavy fire at a few yards
range. The 2-4th N.I. was pushed up to reinforce them, and two
12 prs. sent for, with which the gate was blown open ; three successive
gates had to be forced before an entrance into the main fort could
be effected. Once inside the fort, the British troops cleared it out
and some 2,000 Mahrattas were killed. The British casualties were
also heavy, numbering 265 in all, including 6 British officers and
21 Europeans killed, and 11 British officers and 71 Europeans
wounded ; the chief sufferers being the 76th Foot, who lost 9 officers and 66 men, and by whose valour the fortress was captured.
That night Lake received news of the raid on Shekoabad referred to
above, and immediately despatched the 3rd Cavalry Brigade (29th
Light Dragoons, 1st and 4th Bengal Light Cavalry) to repel the
incursion and relieve Shekoabad which was held by five companies
1-11th N.I. with one gun 2-1st Battalion Artillery.

The 1-4th N.I. was left to garrison Allighur, and without waiting
to strengthen his weakened force, Lake pushed on, and on 11th
September, near Delhi, encountered the enemy, 19,000 men with
100 guns, under M. Louis Bourquien who had succeeded Perron as
Scindia's Commander-in-Chief.

The enemy held a strong position with both flanks resting on
swamps ; Lake reconnoitred personally (as was his custom) with the
cavalry, and then slowly retreated masking the approach of his own
infantry and inducing the enemy to advance. The cavalry then
opened out and let the infantry advance, who, in the face of the
heaviest fire, continued their march until within a hundred paces of
the Mahratta line, when they shattered it with a volley and a charge.

The British casualties, including two officers killed by sunstroke,
were 486, of which the European portion was 6 officers and 47 men
killed, 10 officers and 127 men wounded. The 76th Foot again bore
the brunt and, as ever, were the backbone of the army ; their losses
totalled 138. Their commanding officer was Capt. W. Boyes, all
the senior officers having been knocked out at Allighur ; but Major
W. Macleod, though wounded on that occasion, was present at the
Battle of Delhi in his palanquin. The Mahrattas lost 68 guns and
over 3,000 men, and on the 14th September M. Bourquien and other
French officers surrendered as prisoners. The 2-4th and four companies 2-17th N.I. were left in garrison at Delhi ; Lieut.-Colonel
D. Ochterlony, an officer soon to become famous in the annals of the
Indian Army, being appointed Resident. In October, Lake was
reinforced by the arrival of the remainder of his detached troops,

B

including the 8th Light Dragoons; and on the 4th October he commenced operations against Agra, which capitulated on the 17th; the casualties numbered 230, confined to the Staff, Artillery, and Native infantry regiments. The treasure captured in Agra amounted to 22 lakhs of rupees. The 2-2nd N.I. was left to garrison the place, and on 27th October Lake marched with the rest of his men against a large force summoned by Scindia from the Deccan to recover Delhi. On 29th October Lake left all his heavy guns and baggage at Fattehpur Sikri under guard of the 1-2nd and 1-14th N.I. and pushed on by forced marches. He overtook the Mahrattas near Laswaree on 1st November, and attacked them in a heavy dust storm with his cavalry, with indifferent success. When the tired infantry arrived on the field at mid-day, Lake attempted to turn the enemy's right flank, but the Mahrattas changed front with rapidity and ease; and the leading column headed, as usual, by the 76th Foot suffered severely. Led by Lake and Major-General C. Ware they pressed their attack home, and with the aid of the cavalry turned the defeat into a debacle. 7,000 Mahrattas were left dead on the field, and 72 guns were taken. The British casualties numbered 824, 15 British officers and 82 Europeans being killed, and 27 British officers and 282 Europeans being wounded; the 76th Foot contributing no less than 213 to the total. Lake had one or two horses shot under him; while Major-General Ware and Colonel T. P. Vandeleur, commanding the 1st Cavalry Brigade, were killed.

These victories, backed up by those in the Deccan (to which reference will be made later) and minor successes elsewhere, compelled Scindia and Bhoonsla to make peace. But to watch Holkar, Lake detached a column of Native troops under Monson to protect Jeypore, while he himself withdrew to Agra for the coming hot weather.

Monson's operations ended in complete disaster; advancing too far, he was compelled to retreat in the middle of the rains before Holkar's vastly superior forces. The retreat ended in a disordered flight, and the draggled remnants of his force reached Agra on 31st August, 1804, after a constant retreat of 350 miles. This rout compelled Lake to take the field in person once more.

On 1st October Lake marched from Agra, his first objective being Delhi, which was being attacked by Holkar's infantry and artillery. The defence of the city and fortress of Delhi from 7th—15th October by two and a-half battalions of N. Infantry and some 2,000 irregulars (many of whom deserted), was an extraordinary military feat; the more so, as the defenders had no regular artillery. A gallant sortie under Lieut. J. Rose, 2-14th N.I., later Lieut.-General Sir J. Rose, K.C.B., on 9th October, was completely successful, the breaching guns being spiked; and the repulse of an assault on the Lahore Gate on the 14th, combined with news of Lake's advance compelled the enemy to raise the siege. Lake relieved Delhi on the 17th and after strengthening the garrison finally decided to pursue Holkar's immense force of cavalry with his own cavalry, horse artillery and reserve, while Major-General J. H. Fraser with two regiments of native cavalry, the artillery, and three brigades of infantry marched toward Deig against Holkar's infantry and artillery. For nearly three weeks Lake pursued Holkar's cavalry; at last leaving his reserve behind, he marched by night with his six regiments of cavalry and one troop of horse artillery, and surprising Holkar's camp in the morning (17th November) at Farruckabad, defeated him with fearful slaughter. The pursuit continued for miles, and no less than 3,000 Mahrattas were killed, the British losses being 3 men killed, 25 wounded, and 75 casualties among the horses. This crushing defeat finished off Holkar's cavalry; and meanwhile Fraser had finished off his infantry and artillery; reinforced on 10th November by a detachment of the Bengal European Regiment, he attacked the enemy outside the fortress of Deig on the 13th. The 76th Foot, as usual, led the right and leading column; the troops forming for the attack at 3 a.m. The Mahrattas were defeated at all points, at least 2,000 were killed, 87 guns were taken, and the slaughter only ceased at 3 p.m., when the Fortress of Deig, which belonged to the Rajah of Bhurtpore, received the fugitives and opened fire on the British troops with its guns. The British casualties were 652, to which total the 76th contributed 153. General Fraser was mortally wounded, while leading the 76th Foot in the attack, and the command devolved on Monson.

Monson withdrew the army with the captured guns to Muttra, where Lake joined him; and on the 11th December, after the arrival of a battering train, the army marched to the Siege and Capture of Deig. On the 13th the place was invested, and at midnight, 23rd—24th December, the breach was stormed, the 22nd, 76th and Bengal European Regiment forming the bulk of the assaulting troops. The casualties at the successful assault were 225 (and during the siege about 90). The citadel fell the next day, and leaving the 1-4th N.I. in garrison, Lake marched on 28th December to the Siege of Bhurtpore. Although strengthened by the 75th Foot and troops from Bombay, the four assaults delivered in January and February, 1805, were uniformly unsuccessful, due to an insufficient battering train, and want of care and deliberation in the siege. Lake was however undeterred, and the Rajah of Bhurtpore seeing that it would be merely a matter of time, made overtures of peace, which were accepted. The total casualties before Bhurtpore were over 3,000 men; the 76th Foot lost 16 officers and 188 men, and other European regiments fared as badly.

The corps actually present at the foregoing battles, etc., are given below, as also a list of some of the Engineer officers engaged.

B 2

MAHRATTA WAR, 1803–5.

(1). *General G. Lake's Campaign, August, 1803—March, 1804.*

The Grand Army was composed as follows :—

Commander-in-Chief's personal escort, one company, 1-11th Bengal N.I.

Cavalry Division :—Colonel W. St. Leger, 27th Light Dragoons.

1st Brigade :—Colonel T. P. Vandeleur, 8th Light Dragoons.

H.M. 8th Light Dragoons.

1st and 3rd Bengal Light Cavalry.

2nd Brigade :—Colonel W. St. Leger, 27th Light Dragoons (commanding the Division).

H.M. 27th Light Dragoons.

2nd and 6th Bengal Light Cavalry.

3rd Brigade :—Colonel R. Macan, Bengal Cavalry.

H.M. 29th Light Dragoons.

4th Bengal Light Cavalry.

Artillery and Park :—Lieut.-Colonel J. Horsford, Bengal Artillery.

1st, 2nd and 3rd Companies, 1st Battn.

1st, 2nd, 3rd and 4th Companies, 2nd Battn.

Engineers and Pioneers :—Capt. T. Wood, Bengal Engineers.

Infantry :—Right Wing :—Major-General C. Ware, H.E.I.C.S.

1st Brigade :—Lieut.-Colonel Hon. W. Monson, 76th Foot.

H.M. 76th Foot.

1-4th, 2-4th, and 4 Companies 2-17th Bengal N.I.

3rd Brigade :—Colonel J. McDonald, 15th B.N.I.

1-15th, 2-15th, and 2-12th Bengal N.I.

Left Wing :—Major-General Hon. F. St. John, H.M.S.

2nd Brigade :—Colonel E. Clarke, 9th Bengal N.I.

2-8th, 2-9th, 1-12th and 6 Companies 2-16th Bengal N.I.

4th Brigade :—Lieut.-Colonel J. Powell, 8th Bengal N.I.

1-2nd, 2-2nd, 1-14th Bengal N.I.

Troops Present at the Storm of Allighur, 4th September, 1803.

2 Brigades of Cavalry, brigaded as under :—

2nd Brigade :—H.M. 27th Light Dragoons, 2nd and 3rd Bengal Light Cavalry.

3rd Brigade :—H.M. 29th Light Dragoons, 1st and 4th Bengal Light Cavalry.

Artillery, Engineers and Pioneers.

1st, 3rd, and 4th Infantry Brigades, as given above.

The 1st Infantry Brigade, with details of artillery, etc., were alone actively engaged, though the 27th Light Dragoons also sustained slight casualties.

Casualties :— 6 British officers and 21 Europeans killed.

11 ,, ,, 71 ,, wounded.

Total casualties, including Natives, 265.

N.B.—The 8th Light Dragoons were on the march up from Cawnpore, the 6th Bengal Light Cavalry were in charge of a convoy marching to join the army, and the 2nd Infantry Brigade was detached near Anupshahr.

Early on 5th September Colonel Macan with the 3rd Cavalry Brigade (29th Light Dragoons, 1st and 4th Bengal Light Cavalry) was ordered to Shekoabad to repel an incursion into the provinces ; the 1-4th Bengal N.I. was left in garrison at Allighur, and the army (thus reduced) moved forward.

Troops Present at the Battle of Delhi, 11th September, 1803.

The 2nd Cavalry Brigade :—H.M. 27th Light Dragoons, 2nd and 3rd Bengal Light Cavalry.

Artillery, Engineers and Pioneers.

The 1st Infantry Brigade, less the 1-4th Bengal N.I.

The 3rd and 4th Infantry Brigades.

The 4 Companies 2-17th Bengal N.I. (1st Brigade) formed the camp guard and sustained no casualties.

The 6th Bengal Light Cavalry, with its convoy, got into touch with the rear guard of the army on the evening of the 10th September, and remained on the 11th September in charge of this convoy ; but survivors received the clasp for the " Battle of Delhi " in 1851. Total casualties, 486, of which the European losses were 6 officers and 47 men killed, 10 officers and 127 men wounded, and 8 men missing. 68 guns were captured.

The 2-4th and 4 Companies of 2-17th Bengal N.I. were left in garrison at Delhi.

Between the 2nd and 12th October, the 8th Light Dragoons, Macan's Cavalry Brigade (29th Light Dragoons, 1st and 4th Bengal Light Cavalry) and the 2nd Infantry Brigade (Colonel E. Clarke) joined the army ; and the cavalry being now united was brigaded as shown on page 20 ; Colonel T. P. Vandeleur succeeded St. Leger as senior cavalry officer, when the latter quitted the army on 27th October.

After the capitulation of Agra, 17th October, 1803, the 2-2nd Bengal N.I. was left in garrison there, and on 29th October the 1-2nd and 1-14th Bengal N.I. were left at Fatehpur Sikri with the heavy guns (probably 2nd, 3rd, and 4th Companies, 2nd Battalion Artillery) and baggage.

Troops Present at Laswaree, 1st November, 1803.

The 3 Cavalry Brigades (8 regiments).

Artillery (less the Companies at Fatehpur Sikri), Engineers, Pioneers.

Infantry, H.M. 76th Foot, and the 2nd and 3rd Infantry Brigades.

The casualties were 824, of which the European were 15 officers and 82 men killed, 27 officers and 282 men wounded. 72 guns were captured.

Colonel J. McDonald, 15th Bengal N.I., succeeded Major-General C. Ware, and Colonel R. Macan succeeded Colonel T. P. Vandeleur, both these officers having been killed.

The cavalry brigadiers were:—1st Brigade:—Colonel T. P. Vandeleur (and senior officer). 2nd Brigade:—Lieut.-Colonel J. O. Vandeleur. 3rd Brigade :—Colonel R. Macan.

Lieut.-Colonel J. Gordon, 1st Bengal Light Cavalry, succeeded to the command of the 1st Brigade.

(2). *Lake's Campaign, September, 1804—March, 1805.*
Cavalry Division :—Colonel R. Macan.

1st Brigade :—Lieut.-Colonel J. O. Vandeleur, 8th Light Dragoons
   H.M. 8th Light Dragoons.
   2nd, 3rd, 6th Bengal Light Cavalry.

2nd Brigade :—Lieut.-Colonel T. Browne, 2nd Bengal Light Cavalry.
   H.M. 27th and 29th Light Dragoons.
   1st and 4th Bengal Light Cavalry.

Horse Artillery :—*Experimental Troop. Capt. C. Brown.

Infantry Division :—Major-General J. H. Fraser, H.M.S.

1st Brigade :—Lieut.-Colonel Hon. W. Monson, 76th Foot.
   H.M. 76th Foot.
   1-2nd and 1-4th Bengal N.I.

2nd Brigade :—Lieut.-Colonel G. S. Browne, 4th Bengal N.I.
   1-15th, 2-15th, 1-21st Bengal N.I. (6 Companies).

3rd Brigade :—Lieut.-Colonel G. Ball, 8th Bengal N.I.
   1-8th, 2-22nd Bengal N.I. (7 Companies).

Reserve :—Lieut.-Colonel P. Don, 15th Bengal N.I.
   Flank Companies, H.M. 22nd Foot.
   1-12th, 2-12th and 2-21st Bengal N.I.

Artillery :—Lieut.-Colonel J. Horsford.
   1st, 2nd, and 3rd Companies, 1st Battalion.
   1st, 3rd and 4th Companies, 2nd Battalion.

Engineers, Pioneers :—Capt. T. Robertson, Bengal Engineers.

On 1st October Lake marched from Agra, and on the 16th relieved Delhi.

Defence of Delhi, 7th—15th October, 1804.
Resident :—Lieut.-Colonel D. Ochterlony, 12th Bengal N.I
O.C. Troops :—Lieut.-Colonel W. Burn, 2-14th N.I.
Garrison :—2-4th, 2-14th and 4 Companies 2-17th Bengal N.I.
Capt. Harriott's Battalion. ⎫
Lieut. Birch's Battalion. ⎬ Irregular Troops, a number of
Lieut. Scott's Najibs. ⎪   whom deserted.
Irregular levies. ⎭

* Afterwards 1st Troop, 1st Brigade, Bengal Horse Artillery.

The garrison was reinforced by the 1-21st N.I. ; and the 2-14th N.I., with two corps of irregular infantry, marched for Saharanpur, but was attacked by Holkar at Shamli.

On 31st October Lake marched from Delhi to Burn's relief and in pursuit of Holkar with all the cavalry (except the 2nd and 3rd Light Cavalry), the Horse Artillery, and the Reserve under Lieut.-Colonel Don, with six guns and two howitzers. After 16 days' continual marching, Lake left the Reserve and heavy guns behind, and marching by night with his six regiments of cavalry and troop of horse artillery, cut Holkar's army to pieces on the early morning of 17th November. His casualties were only 3 men killed and 25 wounded, so sudden was the surprise and complete the defeat of Holkar.

Meanwhile on 5th November Major-General Fraser marched from Delhi with the 2nd and 3rd Light Cavalry (Lieut.-Colonel T. Browne), the Foot Artillery, 1st, 2nd, and 3rd Infantry Brigades (less the 1-21st N.I. left near Delhi), Engineers, Pioneers and Hearsey's Irregular Cavalry, towards Deig against Holkar's infantry and heavy guns.

On the 10th November he was reinforced by a detachment of the Bengal European Regiment (350 strong) at Goburdan, and early on the 13th November attacked Holkar's army outside the Fortress of Deig.

Troops Present at the Battle of Deig, 13th November, 1804.

Cavalry :—Lieut.-Colonel T. Browne, 2nd L.C.

2nd and 3rd Bengal Light Cavalry.

Artillery :—
Engineers, Pioneers :— $\left. \right\}$ as given above.

Infantry :—1st, 2nd, and 3rd Brigades as given above, less the 1-21st Bengal N.I. and plus the detachment of Bengal European Regiment, added to the 2nd Brigade.

Hearsey's Irregular Cavalry. (The 3rd Brigade was in reserve).

Casualties :—652 in all ; of which 6 British officers and 57 Europeans were killed, 16 British officers and 189 Europeans wounded and 12 missing. Fraser was mortally wounded, and died at Muttra on 24th November. 87 guns were captured.

The Fortress of Deig opened fire on the British, and Monson withdrew the army to Muttra, with the captured guns, where Lake joined him with his troops from Farruckabad on 28th November, and on the 11th December, after the arrival of a battering train, the whole army marched to invest Deig.

Troops Present at the Siege and Capture of Deig, 11th—25th December.

The whole army, as enumerated above, less the 1-21st N.I. The casualties during the siege were about 90, of whom two British officers were killed ; at the assault on 23rd—24th December, they were 225, of whom two other British officers were killed.

Assault on Deig, Midnight, December 23rd—24th, 1804.

Right Column :—Capt. S. Kelly, European Regiment.
　4 Battalion Companies European Regiment.
　5 Companies 1-12th Bengal N.I.

Left Column :—Major J. Radcliffe, 1-12th Bengal N.I.
　4 Battalion Companies European Regiment.
　5 Companies 1-12th Bengal N.I.

Centre Column :—Lieut.-Colonel K. Macrae, 76th Foot.
　Flank Companies H.M. 22nd and 76th Foot, and European
　Regiment, also 1-8th Bengal N.I.

A proportion of artillery, engineers and pioneers accompanied the assaulting columns.

The citadel capitulated on 25th December ; the 1-4th Bengal N.I. and Hearsey's Irregulars were left in garrison at Deig, and Lake marched on to his unsuccessful siege of Bhurtpore.

Casualties in action of the British Infantry :—

	Killed.		Wounded.	
	Offrs.	Men.	Offrs.	Men.
4th Sept., 1803—21st Feb., 1805.　H.M. 76th Foot..	13	177	22	611
23rd Dec., 1804—21st Feb., 1805.　H.M. 22nd Foot (Flankers)	—	33	9	145
23rd Dec., 1804—21st Feb., 1805.　Bengal European Regiment	—	45	14	206

N.B.—Casualties during the investment of Deig are not included, as they are not known.

Average monthly strengths of rank and file :—

	1. 9. 03 to 31. 3. 04.	1. 9. 04 to 31. 3. 05.
H.M.　8th Lt. Dragoons ..	607 men	540 men.
,,　27th ,,　,, ..	358 ,,	321 ,,
,,　29th ,,　,, ..	370 ,,	331 ,,
,,　76th Foot	964 ,,	703 ,,
,,　22nd ,, ...	200 (Flank Cos.)	882 ,, (whole regt.).
Bengal European Regiment ..	588 men	331 ,,

1st MAHRATTA WAR.

An Incomplete List of Engineer Officers engaged.

I. LAKE'S OPERATIONS.

Bengal Engineers.

Capt. Thos. Wood, Commanding Engineer, Storm of Allighur, Battle of Delhi, Capture of Agra, Battle of Laswaree, Reduction of Rampoora (1804).

Capt. Thos. Robertson, Battle of Deig, Siege and Capture of Deig, Siege of Bhurtpore (1805).

Lieut. H. W. Carmichael Smyth, Storm of Allighur, Battle of Delhi, Capture of Agra, Battle of Laswaree, Battle of Deig, Siege and Capture of Deig, Siege of Bhurtpore, Capture of Gohad (1806).

Lieut. Rd. Tickell, Battle of Deig, Siege and Capture of Deig, Siege of Bhurtpore (1805).

Ensign J. H. Jones, Siege of Bhurtpore. Killed at the assault of Fort Kamona, November, 1807.

Bombay Engineers.

Lieut. Wm. Cowper, Siege of Bhurtpore (1805). Chief Engineer with Bombay Force under Major-General Rd. Jones.

II. OPERATIONS IN CUTTACK, UNDER LIEUT.-COLONEL GEO. HARCOURT.

Capt. J. T. Blunt, Bengal Engineers.

Lieut. W. Ravenshaw, Madras Engineers.

III. OPERATIONS IN BROACH UNDER LIEUT.-COLONEL H. WOODINGTON.

Capt. J. Cliffe (or Clift), Bombay Engineers.

OPERATIONS IN THE DECCAN, 1803.

The operations in the Deccan were undertaken by two forces acting in conjunction, viz. :—that commanded by Major-General the Hon. A. Wellesley, and the Hyderabad Subsidiary Force commanded by Colonel Jas. Stevenson, of the Madras Cavalry.

Wellesley's force was portion of an army of observation, 19,000 strong, assembled at Hurryhur on the N.W. Frontier of Mysore in November, 1802, under the command of Lieut.-General J. Stuart.

Wellesley marched from Hurryhur on the 9th March, 1803, through the Mahratta territory *en route* for Poona, and on the 15th April was in touch with Stevenson's force at Akloos on the Neera River.

The composition of the two forces, March, 1803, was as follows :—

Wellesley's Force.

Cavalry :—Colonel T. Dallas, 4th Madras N. Cavalry (succeeded by Lieut.-Colonel P. Maxwell, 19th Light Dragoons, who was killed 23. 9. 03).

H.M. 19th Light Dragoons (412 sabres).

4th, 5th, and 7th Madras N. Cavalry (1,297 sabres).

Artillery :—Capt. M. Beauman, Madras Artillery (108 gunners, 206 Lascars).

Guides :—Ensign G. Rowley, Madras Engineers. (Died 28. 6. 03).

Pioneers :—1st Battn. Madras Pioneers (704 R. & F.). Capt. W. P. Heitland, 6th M.N.I.

1st Infantry Brigade :—Lieut.-Col. W. Harness, H.M. 80th Foot. H.M. Scotch Brigade (1,013 R. & F.). 1-2nd, 2-3rd, and 2-12th Madras N. Infantry (3,003 R. & F.).

2nd Infantry Brigade :—Lieut.-Colonel W. Wallace, H.M. 74th Foot.
    H.M. 74th Foot (754 R. & F.).   1-3rd, 1-8th, and 2-18th
    Madras N. Infantry (3,120 R. & F.).
Attached :—2,400 Mysore Horse ; 3,000 Peishwa's Horse.

Hyderabad Subsidiary Force.

    Colonel Jas. Stevenson, Madras Cavalry.
Cavalry :—Lieut.-Colonel Hon. A. Sentleger, 6th Madras N.C.
    3rd and 6th Madras N. Cavalry (1,018 sabres).
Artillery :—Capt. U. Burke, Madras Artillery (168 gunners,
    310 Lascars).
Pioneers :—2 Companies 2nd Battn. Madras Pioneers (206 R. & F.)
1st Infantry Brigade :—Lieut.-Colonel H. Maclean, 2-9th M.N.I.
    2-2nd, 1-6th and 2-9th Madras N. Infantry (3,849 R. & F.).
2nd Infantry Brigade :—Lt.-Col. J. Haliburton, 2-7th M.N.I.
    2-7th, 1-11th and 2-11th Madras N. Infantry (3,333 R. & F.).
Attached :—7,000 horse, 5,000 infantry, 40 guns, Nizam's Army.

Certain changes were made in the composition of these forces,
which may be noted here :—H.M. 78th Foot sailed to Bombay from
Fort William, and joined Wellesley early in May, replacing the Scotch
Brigade in the 1st Infantry Brigade, which had been transferred to
Stevenson's force on 16th April under orders from Lieut.-General
Stuart.

Poona was reached on the 20th April, just in time to save its
destruction by the Mahrattas, and arrangements were made for the
return of the Peishwa to his capital from Bombay, whither he had
fled ; and a garrison consisting of 5 companies H.M. 84th Foot and
some Native troops installed there.   At this time Wellesley's artillery
was strengthened by the addition of the 3rd and 5th Companies,
Bombay Artillery, and Capt. J. Johnson, Bombay Engineers, joined
his Staff as Chief Engineer.

The first offensive action against Scindiah was the capture of
the town and fort of Ahmednuggar, 8th—11th August, 1803, by
Wellesley's division, 4 British officers and 26 other ranks being
killed, and 2 British officers and 109 other ranks wounded.

The garrison left in Ahmednuggar consisted of a detachment of
artillery, 30 men of H.M. 84th Foot, and the 2-3rd Madras N.
Infantry from Wellesley's 1st Brigade.   The next move was to try
and bring to battle the forces of Scindiah and Berar, which had
invaded the Nizam's territories.   Wellesley had an interview with
Colonel John Collins, recently Resident at Scindiah's court, an
extremely able officer, nicknamed " King " Collins from the regal
pomp which he maintained.   Being an old man of curious appearance
and dress, he excited a good deal of amusement in the young Major-
General, 34 years old, and his Staff.   " King " Collins's parting

piece of advice to Wellesley was, " Well, General, as for their cavalry, you can ride over them, but their guns and their infantry will astonish you." The staff officer, who was present and records this incident, adds that as they rode home laughing at Colonel Collins, they little thought how soon they were to realize the truth of his warning.

The pursuit of Scindiah continued into September, till early on the 23rd September Wellesley was within striking distance of the combined armies of Scindiah and Berar.

The plan had been for Wellesley's and Stevenson's divisions, which were practically in touch with each other, to make independent marches and attack the enemy simultaneously. They had met on the 21st September and arranged for a joint attack early on the 24th. Owing to the confusion that occurred between the name of the village and the district of Bokerdun, the unexpected difficulty of the country which Stevenson had to traverse, and the attack being commenced by Wellesley on the 23rd, this plan miscarried. Stevenson's force was unable to come into action at all, and Wellesley hardly gained the victory of Assye at the cost of nearly one-fourth of his force. Scindiah's artillery and regular infantry fully justified the opinion that Collins had expressed ; their drill and fire discipline almost turned the scale against the British.

The enemy were found to be in line behind the Kaitna River, close to its junction with the Juah River, which was in their rear ; and Wellesley, making a flank march from the right to the left of the enemy's front, determined to attack their left flank, as he judged from the relative positions of two villages (Peepulgaon and Waroor) that there must be a ford across the Kaitna at this point.

This proved to be the case, but while this was going on, the enemy changed front to their left with rapidity and precision, and Wellesley's force was shut up in the narrow V formed by the junction of the Kaitna and the Juah, with the enemy in line across the top of the V, from river to river, their left flank resting on Assye.

The right of the line, consisting of the picquets of the previous night, followed by the 74th Foot, led the attack directly on to the village of Assye, which was held strongly by the enemy. This attack was in a direction towards their right front, and was led by Lieut.-Colonel Wm. Orrok, 1-8th M.N.I., the officer commanding the picquets. Wellesley (who had intended the attack to be clear of Assye) acknowledged that it was impossible for any man to lead troops into a hotter fire than was done by Colonel Orrok, whose name he himself does not disclose ; and the results justify the statement. With the exception of the 1-2nd M.N.I. which remained in rear with the baggage guard, the losses of the picquets are lumped with their regiments, but the casualties of the picquet of the 1-2nd M.N.I. amounted to 21 killed, 22 wounded and 3 missing, out of a strength of about 50. The 74th which supported the picquets lost 11 officers, and 113.men killed, and 6 officers and 271 men wounded, a total of 401 casualties out of about 550 of all ranks. The right of the British line was practically destroyed by the fire of the enemy's artillery which was massed on this flank.

The British attack formation was one of two lines of infantry with the cavalry in reserve in the third line ; the artillery was posted in the intervals between the regiments. The cavalry did good service during the day by their brilliant charges, and lost their brigadier, Lieut.-Colonel P. Maxwell, 19th Light Dragoons, toward the close of the battle in a final but unsuccessful charge. The advance of the centre and left of the British line was unchecked, the 78th Foot being on the left, and the line wheeled round to the right, pivoted on their shattered right and the village of Assye.

The enemy's artillery, being drawn by bullocks, was captured during the advance, but many of the Mahratta gunners remained by their guns prone on the earth and had the audacity to open fire again on the rear of the advancing British line, after the infantry had passed over them, and inflicted great damage. A considerable part of their infantry left the field in unbroken order, across the Juah, but the loss of their guns, 102 pieces in all, was a serious one; seven stand of colours were also captured. The British casualties numbered 428 killed, and 1,138 wounded, no less than 53 British officers being among them. The numbers under fire were about 6,000 rank and file ; these figures do not include the irregular cavalry which lost only one man that day.

The 1-3rd and the 2-18th M.N.I. were not present at the battle, as they had been sent towards Poona on the 20th September, three days before ; while on the other hand the 1-4th and 1-10th M.N.I., which had been despatched with convoys by Lieut.-General Stuart at different dates, were both engaged. The 2-3rd M.N.I. was of course absent, as it had been left at Ahmednuggar.

The losses among the *personnel* of Wellesley's artillery were so heavy that it had to be immediately strengthened by drafts from Stevenson's force. His division was also too shattered by its losses to be able to make any pursuit, a duty which devolved on Stevenson.

The force defeated at Assye was composed of 16 regular battalions (10,500 men) trained by Europeans, and in a small measure officered by them, with over 100 well-equipped and well-served pieces of artillery, in addition to a large number of irregular infantry and cavalry, presumably about as useful on the battlefield as the British irregular allies. The comparative merits of the two armies may probably be judged by the respective strengths of their regular troops engaged in the battle, and there is no doubt that the enemy's artillery was first-rate. The baggage guard declared that the fire of the enemy's guns was maintained with a regularity and persistence resembling the firing of regular infantry.

On the 21st October the fortress of Asseerghur surrendered to Colonel Stevenson for a consideration. The British casualties were 2 killed and 6 wounded, and it is extraordinary that this occasion should have been commemorated by a special clasp in 1851, and the more so when it is remembered that in 1819 it stood a prolonged siege by the British who sustained heavy losses in reducing it. It is interesting to note that in 1851 several survivors of the Siege of Asseerghur in 1819, put in claims for the clasp for 1803.

On the 22nd October the 1-3rd M.N.I. rejoined Wellesley, as he had sent to recall it three days after the battle of Assye ; and the united forces of Wellesley and Stevenson came into contact with the diminished forces of the enemy on the plains of Argaum, 29th November, 1803.

The British troops engaged consisted of Wellesley's division that had fought at Assye, plus the 1-3rd M.N.I. which had been recalled since, and the whole of Stevenson's division as given above, including H.M. Scotch Brigade (94th Foot). (N.B.—There is some doubt as to whether the 5th Company, Bombay Artillery, was still with Wellesley's division).

The enemy were in line, infantry and guns in the centre, flanked by cavalry and light troops ; the British were in two lines, infantry in front, and cavalry in echelon on the flanks.

The attack was delayed owing to two Native regiments of Wellesley's division, which had lost a large number of their British officers at Assye, falling into confusion early in the fight. This necessitated Wellesley rallying and re-forming them in person, which he effected most skilfully without hurting their *amour propre* by pretending to imagine that they had misunderstood their orders. H.M. 74th and 78th were attacked by a large body of " Persian " troops, who were destroyed entirely, and the 1-6th M.N.I. having repulsed Scindiah's cavalry on our left, the enemy's line was broken and retired in disorder, leaving 38 guns and all their ammunition in the victors' hands. The cavalry took up the pursuit till late at night.

Whether by accident or design, Lieut.-Colonel Orrok, the fire-eater of Assye, was with his regiment on baggage guard on this occasion. Colonel Stevenson, who was a most capable officer but in a bad state of health, commanded his division in action from the back of an elephant, an unusual mount for a British divisional commander.

The British casualties numbered 346, nearly one half being sustained by the few British corps ; the 74th Foot having 52.

The combined British force marched at once to the siege of the fortress of Gawilghur, which was stormed on 15th December after a nine days' siege, during which the British casualties numbered 126. The troops engaged were the same units as those present at Argaum.

These successes, combined with those of Lake, broke up the con-federacy, and compelled Scindiah and Berar to sue for peace, which was concluded early in 1804, and it will be remembered that Lake's campaign of 1804, which has been recounted before, was directed against Holkar, and later against Bhurtpoor.

Incomplete List of Engineer Officers engaged in the War.

Capt. Jno. Johnson, Bombay Engineers, Chief Engineer with Wel-lesley. Joined at Dharwar. Siege and Capture of Ahmed-nuggar, Battles of Assye and Argaum, Siege and Capture of Gawilghur, Chandore and Gaulna.

Ensigns G. Rowley, Madras Engineers, commanded the Guides. Died 28. 6. 03. J. Blakiston, Madras Engineers, Siege and Capture of Ahmednuggar, Battles of Assye and Argaum, Siege and Capture of Gawilghur. Sam. Russell, Madras Engineers, with Hyderabad Subsidiary Force, Reduction of Asseerghur, Battle of Argaum, Siege and Capture of Gawilghur.

The Nepaul War, 1814–16.

The Nepaul War, occasioned by the encroachments and insolence of the Nepalese, consisted of two distinct phases, the first from October, 1814—May, 1815, and the second from December, 1815—March, 1816.

The first phase of the war was carried out by four divisions (and various detached forces), acting somewhat independently on an extremely extended frontier. They were as follows :—

3rd or N.W. Division.

Colonel D. Ochterlony in command.

2-1st, 2-6th, 1-19th and 6 Companies 2-19th Bengal N.I. (Colonel J. Arnold).

Artillery :—Detachment (Major A. McLeod).

Pioneers :—3rd and 4th Companies.

Cavalry :—2nd Bengal Cavalry, 1 rissala Skinner's Horse.

Reserve :—2-3rd Bengal N.I. and Light Battalion (formed from corps of the Division).

Reinforcements :—2-7th, detachment of 1-14th, and 1-15th Bengal N.I., Nusseeree Ghurkas and Sikh levy.

Original strength, 5,993 ; augmented to 7,112 ; irregulars, 4,463.

2nd Division.

Major-General R. Gillespie (killed at Kalunga 31. 10. 14). Colonel S. Mawbey (temporarily). Major-General G. Martindell (succeeded 20. 12. 14).

Detachment H.M. 8th Light Dragoons. H.M. 53rd Foot. Detachment Bengal Horse Artillery and Foot Artillery (Capt.-Lieut. W. Battine). 5th and 6th Companies Pioneers. 7th Bengal Cavalry, and 1 rissala Skinner's Horse. 1-6th, 1-17th and 4 Companies 2-19th Bengal N.I.

Reserve :—1-7th B.N.I. and Light Battn. (Light Companies of 1-6th, 1-7th, 1-17th, 2-16th, 2-26th, 1-1st, 1-5th and 1-27th B.N.I.).

Reinforcements :—1-13th, 4 Companies 1-27th, 2-26th, 2-27th and Light Company 1-26th B.N.I., also 10th B.N.I.

Original strength, 3,513 ; augmented to 10,422 ; irregulars, 6,688.

Benares Division.

Major-General J. S. Wood.

H.M. 17th Foot. Left Wings 1-14th and 2-14th B.N.I. and 2-17th B.N.I.

Artillery :—Capt.-Lieut. J. MacDowell, and later Capt. G. Pollock. 8th Company Pioneers. 8th Bengal Cavalry and 1 Troop 6th Bengal Cavalry.

Reserve :—4 Companies 2-8th B.N.I., Grenadier Companies 1-17th and 2-17th B.N.I., 4 Companies 2-12th B.N.I.

Reinforcements :—Right Wing 1-14th B.N.I.

Original strength, 4,494 ; augmented to 4,698 ; irregulars, 900.

Dinapore Division.

Major-General B. Marley, succeeded by Major-General G. Wood.

H.M. 24th Foot.

1-8th, 1-18th, 2-15th, 2-25th and Left Wing 2-22nd B.N.I.

Ramgurh Battalion.

Detachment Chumparun L.I.

⎫ Two brigades commanded by Lieut.-Colonel T. Chamberlain, 24th Foot, and Lieut.-Colonel G. Dick, 9th B.N.I. ⎭

Artillery :—Major G. Mason.

Pioneers :—1st, 2nd and 7th Companies (Capt. J. Swinton). Gardner's Irregular Horse.

Reinforcements :—H.M. 14th and 17th Foot, and detachment Bengal European Regiment, 1-12th B.N.I., 2 Companies 1-25th and 4 Companies 1-9th B.N.I. Patna Provincial Battn., Chumparun L.I. Dromedary Corps.

Original strength, 7,989 ; augmented strength, 13,424.

Tirhoot Frontier.

Major P. Bradshaw.

Dets. Gardner's Horse, 2-5th, 2-15th B.N.I. and Chumparun L.I.

North Frontier, East of the Koosi.

Capt. B. Latter.

Rungpore and Patna Provincial Battalions ; detachments of 1-9th, 1-18th, 2-21st B.N.I. and of the Purnea Provincial Battalion. Detachment Artillery.

Original strength, 2,218 ; augmented strength, 2,723.

Kumaon.

Colonel W. L. Gardner, succeeded by Colonel J. Nicolls.
1-4th, 2-4th, 2-5th and Grenadier Company of 2-27th B.N.I. Flank
Battalion from the Dhun. Rohilcund Irregulars. Corps of Pathan
or Mewatti Infantry.

The achievements of these various forces were as follows :—

Gillespie fell in a futile attack on Kalunga on 31st October, 1814 ;
Colonel Mawbey who succeeded him made a second unsuccessful
assault, sustaining even heavier losses than at the first ; but the
fort was evacuated finally by the Ghurkas.

Major-General Martindell (who was appointed to the command
vice Gillespie killed) carried out some very unsuccessful operations
against the Fort of Jyetuck, and having sustained severe losses
settled down to blockade the place, which was evacuated in 1815 on
account of Ochterlony's successes elsewhere.

Major-General J. S. Wood made an unsuccessful attack on the
post of Jeetpore, withdrew his forces, and contented himself with a
passive defence and some futile demonstrations. His force returned
to cantonments in May, 1815.

Major-General Marley's force lost two advanced posts held by
detachments, which were attacked and defeated with heavy loss.
These disasters unnerved General Marley to such an extent that,
despite strong reinforcements, which included two King's regiments,
he *deserted his division* early on February 10th, 1815, without warning
or handing over. Colonel G. Dick assumed command at this crisis,
until the arrival of Major-General G. Wood from Calcutta. General
G. Wood proved as inactive as other commanders and effected
nothing.

Ochterlony began his operations in November, 1814, and direct-
ing them against Nalaghur, Ramghur, and Mallown, with skill
and decision, took the enemy's positions one by one, until the
principal position at Mallown fell on 11th May, 1815 ; this led to the
fall of Jyetuck as mentioned above. His division was the only
one handled with skill, and which achieved its object, and for his
valuable services he received deservedly the K.C.B. and was created
a baronet.

The minor operations conducted by Latter, Bradshaw, and
Nicolls were generally successful, and Nicolls captured Almora.
The Nepalese Government then entered into negotiations, which
lasted many months, but towards the end of the year it was discovered that they did not intend to ratify the treaty that had been
agreed upon. This led to the second phase of the war, and Sir D.
Ochterlony was directed to resume military operations and was
placed in chief command of the invading force.

2nd Phase.—December, 1815—*March,* 1816. *Major-General Sir D. Ochterlony in Command.*

Right Column :—Colonel W. Kelly, 24th Foot.
1st Brigade :—H.M. 24th Foot. 1-18th and Right Wing of 1-21st and Left Wing of 2-21st B.N.I. Chumparun Light Infantry. Strength 4,200.

Centre Column :—Sir D. Ochterlony.
3rd Brigade:—Lieut.-Colonel F. Miller, 87th Foot. H.M. 87th Foot. 2-12th, 2-22nd, and 2-25th B.N.I.
4th Brigade :—Col. G. Dick, succeeded by Lt.-Col. J. Burnett. 2-4th, 2-8th, 2-9th, 2-15th and Right Wing of 1-30th B.N.I. Strength 7,843.

Left Column :—Lieut.-Colonel C. Nicoll, 66th Foot.
2nd Brigade :—H.M. 66th Foot. 5th and 8th Grenadier Battalions B.N.I. 1-8th and 2-18th B.N.I. Strength, 4,280.
Attached to the main army and distributed amongst the brigades :—
Artillery, Engineers, 2 Companies Pioneers, and 5 rissalas of the 1st Rohilla Cavalry. Strength 3,070.

Colonel J. Nicoll's Division :—Seetapore and Kumaon.

Artillery, Engineers and 6th Company Pioneers.
Wing of H.M. 67th Foot. 2-10th, 1-22nd, 1-25th and 4th Grenadier Battn. B.N.I. Light Companies 1-1st, 1-2nd, 2-2nd, 1-11th, 1-15th and 2-24th B.N.I.
2nd Rohilla Cavalry (6 rissalas).
Detachment Sirmoor Battn. and half 72nd Experimental Dromedary Corps. Strength 6,617.

Major-General J. S. Wood's Division :—Goruckpore Frontier.

Artillery.
H.M. 17th Foot. Detachments 1-14th and 2-14th B.N.I., 2-17th B.N.I. Detachment Mirzapore Battn. Goruckpore Hill Corps, and Gardner's Horse (2 rissalas). Strength 4,866.
Additions :—2-8th, 2-12th, 5th Grenadier Battn. and detachment 2-17th B.N.I. Detachments Mirzapore Battn. Goruckpore Hill Corps and Artillery. Strength 5,143.

Tityala.

Capt. B. Latter.
Artillery.
Detachments 1-9th, 1-30th and 2-30th B.N.I. and Rungpore Battn. Strength 2,489.

The campaign was short, sharp and decisive. Sir D. Ochterlony advancing in February with the centre column, turned the enemy's position at the Chiriagati Pass, by a difficult and brilliant flank march, defeated them with heavy loss, and occupied Muckwanpore.

c

The right and left columns also advanced, but only the right column experienced any serious fighting in the capture of Fort Hariharpur. The British successes led to another treaty being drawn up, and this time signed, by which the Nepaul Government ceded even more territory than had been demanded in the first treaty. For these brilliant services Ochterlony received the G.C.B., the first officer of the Indian Army to be thus honoured. The company's medal for the war was given in silver to all Native officers and to such Native non-commissioned officers and men who were recommended for the distinction, who had actually served in the hills.

In 1851 the Army of India Medal and clasp " Nepaul " was granted to all survivors, European and Natives (other than those Natives who had received the Company's medal), who had served *in the field*.

This excluded certain troops from the grant, and the European regiments thus excluded were the 14th Foot and the detachment of the Bengal European Regiment, who formed part of the reinforcements ordered up to strengthen the Dinapore (Major-General Marley's) Division in January, 1815.

The British regiments that received the medal and clasp were

Detachment 8th Light Dragoons,

H.M. 17th Foot, 24th Foot, 53rd Foot, 66th Foot, one wing of the 67th Foot, and the 87th Foot,

of whom the 17th and 24th Foot alone served in both phases of the war ; while the 87th Foot took a conspicuous part in the brilliant operations that brought it to a successful conclusion.

An Incomplete List of Officers of the Bengal Engineers who served in the War.

Captains H. W. Carmichael Smith. (With Colonel Mawbey's Column, 1814–15). R. Tickell. R. Smith.

Lieuts. E. Garstin. (1814–15 Campaign). P. Lawtie. (With Ochterlony's division. Died from fatigue 4. 5. 15. A most distinguished junior officer). W. E. Morrison. (With Major-General J. S. Wood's division. Died of wounds 6. 1. 15). J. Peckett.

Ensign G. Hutchinson.

THE SECOND MAHRATTA WAR, 1817–19.

This war was occasioned by the intrigues among the Mahratta rajahs, the lawless and anarchical condition of Central India, and the appalling depredations of the hordes of freebooters known as Pindarris.

The Governor-General, Lord Hastings, determined to suppress these marauders who had become a serious menace. Numbering nearly 20,000, and composed almost exclusively of mounted men, they moved with astonishing rapidity, committing the most unspeakable atrocities as they swept along, and at last they even dared to invade British territory. They were undoubtedly countenanced by some of the Mahratta rajahs, who received a portion of their plunder, and to meet the serious evils that had arisen, the Governor-General mobilized a force of over 100,000 troops, consisting of 13,000 European and 74,000 Native Regulars, 20,000 Irregular Cavalry officered by British officers, and 10,000 Native Irregulars. The artillery numbered 282 guns with the Regulars, and 13 with the Native Irregulars.

The combined military force of the Pindarris and those Mahratta rajahs who could not be trusted, totalled over 200,000 men with 589 guns ; the mounted portion being no less than 130,000 of this total. As the event proved the British troops had to fight the principal Mahratta princes, as well as exterminate the Pindarris.

The British Army, drawn from every presidency, was brigaded on paper as follows :—

The Grand Army (Bengal Presidency).

C.-in-C. :—The Governor-General, Lord Hastings.

1st or Centre Division :—Major-General Thos. Brown.
2nd or Right Division :—Major-General R. S. Donkin.
3rd or Left Division :—Major-General D. Marshall.
Reserve Division :—Major-General Sir D. Ochterlony, G.C.B.

The Army of the Dekkan (Madras and Bombay Presidencies).

C.-in-C. :—Lieut.-General Sir T. Hislop (C.-in-C., Madras).

1st or Advanced Division :—Lieut.-General Sir T. Hislop.
2nd or Hyderabad Division :—Brig.-General J. Doveton.
3rd Division :—Brig.-General Sir J. Malcolm, K.C.B., K.L.S.
4th or Poona Division :—Brig.-General L. Smith, C.B.
5th or Nagpore Division :—Lieut.-Colonel J. W. Adams, C.B.
Reserve Division :—Brig.-General T. Munro (Brig.-General T. Pritzler, 2nd in command).

The Goozerat Division (Bombay Presidency).

Major-General Sir W. T. Keir, K.M.T.

The fighting that occurred between November, 1817, and May, 1819, was of a most extensive and arduous character. The opening of the campaign was signalized by sudden attacks on the small British garrisons at Kirkee and Nagpore by the Regular troops of the Peishwa and the Bhonsla ; while the Army of Holkar met its fate on the banks of the Sipra at the hands of Sir T. Hislop and Sir J. Malcolm in December, 1817. Numberless fortresses were besieged and taken, the Pindarris were exterminated, and the final crushing

C 2

of the Mahratta confederacy effected at the cost of hard fighting and heavy losses.

The following notes will be confined chiefly to those events, which were commemorated in 1851 by clasps to the Army of India Medal, as follows :—

(i.). The Battle of Kirkee, 5th November, 1817, caused by the Peishwa's attack on the garrison of Kirkee.

(ii.). The Battle and Capture of Poona, 11th—16th November, 1817, when the Kirkee troops reinforced by Brig.-General L. Smith, defeated the Peishwa again and took his capital.

(iii.). The Defence of Corygaum, 1st January, 1818, when a detachment of all arms, 900 strong, held the village of Corygaum against the flower of the Peishwa's army, defeated with heavy loss every attack, and withdrew in good order and safety to Sirur.

(iv.). The Battle of Seetabuldee, 26th—27th November, 1817, where the small garrison of Nagpore, seizing the hills of Seetabuldee, withstood the sudden onslaught of the overwhelming forces of the Rajah and beat them off after a fight lasting 18 hours.

(v.). The Battle and Capture of Nagpore, 16th December and 24th—30th December, 1817. These events were the sequel to the Battle of Seetabuldee, in the same way as the Battle and Capture of Poona was the sequel to the Battle of Kirkee. It has to be recorded however with regret that the assault on 24th December failed, and that Nagpore capitulated on terms on 30th December.

(vi.). The Battle of Maheidpoor, 21st December, 1817, when Sir T. Hislop (with Sir J. Malcolm as 2nd in command) defeated Holkar's Army on the banks of the Sipra.

I. OPERATIONS NEAR POONA.

Troops Present at the Battle of Kirkee, 5th November, 1817.

Lieut.-Colonel C. B. Burr, 1-7th Bo. N.I., in command.

    *Detachment H.M. 65th Foot.

    3-2nd Battn. Bombay Artillery (4 guns).

    Bombay European Regiment.

    *The Resident's Escort (2 Companies N.I.).

    2-1st, 2-6th and 1-7th Bo. N.I.

    1st Dapuri Battn., with 3 field guns (Poona Auxiliary Force).

    *Detachment of Pioneers.

    Casualties :—19 killed, 67 wounded.

A wing of 2-6th N.I. with details was left in post at Kirkee. In a few days reinforcements arrived under Brigadier L. Smith, who attacked the Peishwa and captured Poona.

* These corps sustained no casualties.

Troops Present at the Battle and Capture of Poona, 11th—16th November, 1817.

Brigadier L. Smith, 65th Foot, in command.

Right Wing :—Brigadier L. Smith.

H.M. 65th Foot.

*1st Troop Bo. Horse Artillery.

A Flank Battalion (formed from the N.I. regiments present).

*1-2nd, 1-3rd, and *2-9th Bo. N. Infantry.

Left Wing :—Lieut.-Colonel C. J. Milnes, 65th Foot.

Bombay European Regiment.

3-2nd Battn. Bo. Artillery.

The Resident's Escort (2 companies N.I.).

*2-1st, 2-6th, 1-7th Bo. N. Infantry.

Light Company 1-4th Bo. N. Infantry.

Also present, detachments of E and F Companies 2nd Battn. Madras and 3rd and 4th Companies Bombay Pioneers, and Corps of Poona Auxiliary (Irregular) Horse, under Capt. W. Spiller.

Casualties among the Regular troops, 15 killed, 79 wounded.

62 guns were taken.

Troops Present at the Defence of Corygaum, 1st January, 1818.

Whilst marching with a detachment from Sirur to strengthen the garrison of Poona, Capt. F. F. Staunton, 2-1st Bo. N.I., encountered the Peishwa's Army ; seizing the village of Corygaum he held it against all attacks, and though heavy losses were sustained he succeeded in withdrawing his force by night in safety to Sirur.

Troops engaged :—

Auxiliary Horse (250 to 300 men).

Detachment G Company 1st Battn. Madras Artillery (two 6-prs., 25 Europeans and 18 Lascars).

2-1st Bombay N.I. (500 to 550 men).

Casualties :—

Madras Artillery :—13 Europeans and 5 Natives killed, 9 Europeans and 6 Natives wounded.

2-1st Bo. N.I. :—53 killed and 134 wounded.

Auxiliary Horse :—96 casualties.

Of the eight British officers present, three were killed and two wounded.

For their gallantry the 2-1st Bo. N.I. were constituted Grenadiers, and Capt. Staunton was made A.D.C. to the Governor-General, and presented by the H.E.I.C. with a sword of honour and 500 guineas ; he was also nominated C.B. in due course. A monument was erected at the site in 1821 to commemorate the action, inscribed with the names of all who lost their lives in it.

* These corps sustained no casualties.

II. OPERATIONS NEAR NAGPORE AND MAHEIDPOOR.

The small force at Nagpore, under Lieut.-Colonel H. S. Scott, was attacked suddenly by the Rajah's forces, while taking position on the two hills of Seetabuldee outside the town.

Troops Present at the Battle of Seetabuldee, 26th—27th November, 1817.

Lieut.-Colonel H. S. Scott, 1-24th M.N.I., in command.

Troops present :—

6th Bengal Cavalry (3 troops).
Detachment Madras Bodyguard.
    ,,   Madras Artillery (from D Company, 2nd Battn., four 6-prs.).
Detachment Madras Pioneers, 1st Battn.
1-20th and 1-24th Madras N.I.
Residents' Escort (2 Companies N.I.).
Battalion Nagpore Subsidiary Force.

| Casualties. | | | | | | Field State 26th November, 1817. | | | | | |
| Natives. | | | Europeans. | | Corps. | British Officers. | Native Officers. | Other Ranks. | Recruits, Armed. | Recruits, Unarmed. | Recruit Boys. |
Missing.	Wounded.	Killed.	Wounded.	Killed.							
—	22	22	2	I	6th Ben. Cav. . .	5	9	286	—	—	—
—	—	—	—	—	Bodyguard . . .	—	I	17	—	—	—
—	9	2	7	3	Artillery . . .	I	2	52	—	—	—
—	46	15	3	I	1-20th M.N.I. . .	12	11	429	80	—	64
—	98	56	4	2	1-24th M.N.I. . .	9	13	510	80	—	60
4	32	10	I	—	Escort . . .	3	3	173	—	—	—
—	13	8	2	—	Nagpore Battn. . .	4	11	13	70	392	—
—	—	—	—	I	Pioneers, Staff & Details	not given.			—	—	—

N.B.—At this period the Madras Bodyguard consisted of details borne on the strengths of the regiments of cavalry from which they were drawn.

The Resident's escort consisted of 2 Companies Bengal N.I. formed of volunteers from regiments quartered at Barrackpore. For its gallantry the 1-24th M.N.I. was restored to its old position and number, viz. : the 1-1st M.N.I. which it had forfeited for its mutiny at Vellore in 1806.

Battle and Capture of Nagpore.

The troops at Seetabuldee were relieved by the arrival of Brigadier J. Doveton's division, and on the 16th December, 1817, the Battle of Nagpore was fought in which 75 guns and 40 elephants were taken. Nagpore was then invested and an unsuccessful assault delivered on 24th December. Negotiations ensued and the fortress capitulated on 30th December.

Troops Present at the Battle of Nagpore, 16th December, 1817.

Brigadier J. Doveton in command.

Cavalry Brigade :—Lieut.-Colonel R. Gahan, 6th Ben. Cavalry.
Detachment Madras Horse Artillery (6 guns).
6th Bengal Cavalry.
6th Madras Cavalry.

1st Infantry Brigade :—Lieut.-Colonel N. McLeod, 1st Foot.
H.M. 1st Foot (6 Companies).
1-12th Madras N.I., 1-22nd Bengal N.I. and Flank Companies 1-2nd Madras N.I.

2nd Infantry Brigade :—Lieut.-Colonel N. McKellar, 1st Foot.
1 Company H.M. 1st Foot.
2-24th Madras N.I.
Detachment Madras H. Artillery (2 guns).

3rd Infantry Brigade :—Lieut.-Colonel H. S. Scott, 1-24th M.N.I.
1 Company H.M. 1st Foot.
A, C, D Companies Madras Foot Artillery, 2nd Battn.
Detachment Madras Sappers and 1st Battn. Pioneers.
1-11th Madras N.I.
Detachment 2-14th Madras N.I. (1 officer and 70 men).

In support, 2-13th Madras N.I. from 1st Brigade. Principal Reserve Battery (from 2nd Battn. Madras Artillery, A, C, D Companies).

In rear, Berar Brigade (Artillery, Cavalry, and Infantry).—Major R. Pitman, 6th Bengal N.I.

With the baggage 1-20th and 1-24th Madras N.I.

Total casualties from 16th to 24th December inclusive, 94 killed and 348 wounded.

The above troops also effected the capture of Nagpore later on.

Troops Present at the Battle of Maheidpoor, 21st December, 1817.
(The Defeat of Holkar).

Lieut.-General Sir T. Hislop, C.-in-C., the Army of the Dekkan, in command.

Troops present :—
Horse Artillery Brigade :—Capt. H. T. Rudyard, Madras H.A.
1st and 2nd Troops Madras H.A.
Rocket Troop Madras Artillery.
Gallopers 3rd and 8th Madras Cavalry.

1st Cavalry Brigade :—Lieut.-Colonel J. Russell, 3rd Madras N.C.
  1 squadron H.M. 22nd Light Dragoons (100 men).
  3rd Madras Cavalry.
2nd Cavalry Brigade :—Major G. L. Lushington, 4th Madras N.C.
  4th Madras Cavalry.
  8th Madras Cavalry.
Artillery :—Major J. Noble, Madras Artillery.
  D and E Companies 2nd Battn. Madras Artillery.
  Russell Brigade Artillery.
Light Infantry Brigade :—Major H. Bowen, 16th Madras N.I.
  Madras Rifle Corps (4 Companies).   .
  1-3rd and 1-16th M.N.I.
1st Infantry Brigade :—Lieut.-Colonel R. Scott, Madras European
    Regiment.
  Flank Companies H.M. 1st Foot (7 officers, 161 men).
  Madras European Regiment (5 companies, 9 officers, 314 men).
  1-14th and 2-14th Madras N.I.
2nd Infantry Brigade :—Lieut.-Colonel A. M'Dowell, 6th Madras
    N.I.
  2-6th Madras N.I.
  1st and 2nd Battns. of Russell Brigade (Capt. A. Hare, 7th
    Bombay N.I.).
  Detachment 22nd Bengal N.I. (16 men attached to Russell
    Brigade).
  Madras Pioneers, 4 Companies 1st Battn. (B, E, F, G Com-
    panies). Capt. R. M'Craith, 22nd Madras N.I.
  Mysore Silladar Horse, Capt. J. Grant, 5th Madras Cavalry.
  Sir J. Malcolm's Escort (19 men of 6th Madras Cavalry).
  Bhopal Contingent and Nizam's Reformed Horse.
Casualties :—

British Officers ..	4 killed and	34 wounded.		
Europeans	19	,,	99	,,
Natives	151	,,	471	,,

N.B.—Over 200 of the wounded died subsequently, on account of
the bad medical arrangements. 65 guns and 7 elephants were captured.

No other battles or sieges of the 2nd Mahratta War are commemorated by the Army of India medal clasps, though much addi-
tional fighting took place, some of which was very severe. The
most noteworthy of these latter operations were (i.) the Siege and
Capture of Asseerghur in 1819, by Brigadier J. Doveton's and
Sir J. Malcolm's divisions, the total casualties being 313. The
regular troops engaged numbered over 15,000 and included H.M.
1st Foot, 14th Foot, 30th Foot, 67th Foot and the Madras European
Regiment. When one recalls the fact that a clasp was authorized
for the capitulation of this fortress to Colonel James Stevenson in

1803, when two men were killed and six wounded, the omission of this second successful siege is very curious.

(ii.). The Siege and Storm of Malleygaum in May, 1818, when the casualties were 208, including five British officers killed.

(iii.). The Siege and Storm of Nowah in January, 1819, when 200 casualties were sustained. It is to be noted that " Nowah " is borne as an honorary distinction on the colours and appointments of the Native corps engaged which still survive in the Indian Army (none of H.M. Troops were present) but it was passed over in silence in 1851. The Battles of Kirkee and Poona had a political value far outweighing their military character, and probably were commemorated on that account.

Engineer Officers Engaged, 1817–19.

Royal Engineers.	Services.
Lieut. T. H. Elliot	A.D.C. to Sir T. Hislop. Battle of Seetabuldee. Battle of Maheidpoor (wounded). Capture of Talneir, 27. 2. 18.
	N.B.—This officer was on the staff of his father, the Governor of Madras, and was appointed by Sir T. Hislop to be his 2nd A.D.C. His presence at Seetabuldee was due to chance. It is uncertain whether he was present at the subsequent operations round Nagpore.
Bengal Engineers.	
Major T. Anburey*	Principal Field Engineer, 1st Division.
Capt. H. W. C. Smyth* ..	Field Engineer, 1st Division.
„ Rd. Tickell*	Field Engineer, 3rd Division. Capture of Mundla, April, 1818.
Lieut. J. Taylor	Assistant Field Engineer, 1st Division.
„ J. Peckett	Field Engineer, 3rd Division.
„ J. Cheape	Assistant Field Engineer, 3rd Division. Siege and Capture of Asseerghur, March—April, 1819.
„ J. Colvin	Assistant Field Engineer, 3rd Division.
„ A. Irvine*	Assistant Field Engineer, 1st Division. Siege and Capture of Asseerghur.

* N.B.—These four officers were engaged at the Capture of Fort Hathras, April, 1817.

Bengal Engineers.	Services.
Lieut. E. Garstin	Assistant Field Engineer, 4th Division. Capture of Nagpore, Capture of Taragarh, June, 1818, and Madoorajpoor, July, 1818.
,, J. F. Paton..	Adjutant, 1st Division.
., W. J. O. Hall	Field Engineer, Nagpore (5th) Division. *Army of the Dekkan.*
,, G. Hutchinson*	Assistant Field Engineer, 4th Division.
Ensign T. J. Warlow	Assistant Field Engineer, 3rd Division. Siege and Capture of Asseerghur.

Madras Engineers.	
Lieut. T. Davies	Siege and Capture of Nagpore (wounded), of Rajdeir, and of Trimbuck, April, 1818. Killed at Siege of Malligaum, 18th May, 1818.
,, J. Coventry..	Commanding Engineer at Siege and Capture of Asseerghur.
,, Alex. Anderson	Battle of Maheidpoor. Capture of Talneir (wounded). Siege and Capture of Chanda, May, 1818.
,, Alex. Grant	Siege and Capture of Singhur, February—March, 1818. Capture of Poorunder. Operations south of Kistna, Siege and Capture of Wassoota, Sholapur, May, 1818, and of Copal Droog, May, 1819.
Ensign J. W. Nattes	Siege and Capture of Nagpore (wounded), of Rajdeir and of Trimbuck (on the staff). Killed at the Siege of Malligaum, 29th May, 1818.
,, J. Purton	Battle of Maheidpoor, Capture of Talneir, Siege and Capture of Rajdeir, of Trimbuck, and of Malligaum (wounded), also of Asseerghur.
,, J. Oliphant	Siege and Capture of Nowah, January, 1819, and of Copal Droog, May, 1819.

* N.B.—This officer was engaged at the Capture of Fort Hathras, April, 1817.

PLATE II.

EARLY INDIAN CAMPAIGNS AND THE DECORATIONS AWARDED FOR THEM.

ARMY OF INDIA MEDAL. 1803–26.

Madras Engineers.	Services.
Ensign J. J. Underwood	Siege and Capture of Rajdeir, Trimbuck and Malligaum (wounded).
„ E. Lake	Siege and Capture of Rajdeir, Trimbuck (wounded), Malligaum, Jilpy Amair, January, 1819, and Asseerghur.
„ J. Jenkins	With Doveton's division. Died at Akola, 4th December, 1817.

Bombay Engineers.	
Capt. J. Nutt	Operations near Poona, Siege and Capture of Singhur, Poorunder and Wassoota, March—April, 1818, as Commanding Engineer.
Lieut. T. Remon	Capture of Koaree (wounded), March, 1818.
„ J. McLeod	Operations near Poona, Siege and
„ S. Atthill	Capture of Singhur, Poorunder
„ S. Slight	and Wassoota.
Ensign W. M. Ennis	Killed, 13th November, 1817, at the outbreak of hostilities, whilst surveying near Poona.

The detail of the list of services is probably incomplete in a few cases.

THE 1ST BURMESE WAR, 1824–26.

Owing to the fact that special medals for this war were granted by the H.E.I.C. at its close to all the native ranks who served in it, both in Burma and in Arracan, etc., no native was eligible to the medal and clasp " Ava," when the Army of India Medal was granted in 1851.

The King's troops that served in the war were the 1st, 13th, 38th, 41st, 44th, 45th, 47th, 54th, 87th and 89th Foot. The Europeans in the Company's Service entitled to the medal and clasp " Ava " were the European officers, and N.C.O.'s of the Artillery and various corps, also the 1st Madras European Regiment. It was issued also to survivors of the Royal and Indian Navies, who served in the war.

The 1st Foot served at Nagpore and Maheidpoor also ; and the combination of either of these clasps with that for " Ava " is met with ; as also that of " Nepaul " and " Ava " for the 87th Foot, or " Maheidpoor " and " Ava " for the Madras European Regiment.

Very few of the officers and men of the 13th Foot served in

Afghanistan 1839–42, who had previously served in the Burmese War.

The 44th Foot was destroyed at Cabul in 1842.

The combination in a group of the medals with clasps for "Chrystler's Farm" and "Ava" to men of the 89th Foot, is to be met with occasionally, as also of medals with the clasp for "Java" and clasps for "Assye," etc., to the 78th Foot. The combination of the two clasps "Ava" and "Bhurtpoor" is very uncommon.

300 medals with the clasp "Ava" were issued to the Royal Navy, and 46 to the Indian Marine. The vessels employed (many of them very small) were the following. List probably incomplete :—

Royal Navy.	Indian Marine.
Alligator	Asseerghur
Arachne	Diana
Boadicea	Emma
Champion	Ernaad
Larne	Exeter
Liffey	Hastings
Slaney	Margaret
Sophie	Matchless
Tamar	Nereide
Tees	Pluto
	Sophia
	Teignmouth
	Trusty

A List of Engineer Officers Engaged.
Bengal Engineers.

Capt. J. Cheape.

Lieut. F. Abbott (wounded).

,,   G. B. Thomson (with Brigadier J. W. Morrison's force Arakan).

,,   W. Dickson (wounded).

,,   H. de Budé.

,.   J. Tindall (Adjutant and Quartermaster).

,,   J. Crommelin.

Madras Engineers.

Capt. J. Mackintosh (Chief Engineer,   Invalided, 11. 8. 24 ; died 22. 10. 24).

,,   Alex. Grant (Chief Engineer from 21. 12. 24. Died, 20. 5. 25).

Lieut. G. A. Underwood (Chief Engineer from 21. 5. 25. Wounded).

,,   E. Lake (Adjutant).

,,   A. T. Cotton.

SIEGE AND STORM OF BHURTPORE, 10*th December*, 1825—1*st January*, 1826.

The Siege of Bhurtpore was occasioned by the usurpation of Durjan Sal, on the death of the Rajah.

Sir D. Ochterlony, the Resident at Delhi, began to take the necessary measures, which however were countermanded by the Government of India. The old veteran, distinguished throughout a long career by combined caution and daring in the field and wisdom in council, was so mortified by this rebuff that writing a dignified protest he resigned his post and died a few months later at Meerut. Meanwhile the state of affairs in Bhurtpore went from bad to worse, and the Government were compelled to retrace their steps and justify the measures which Sir D. Ochterlony had commenced, immediately after his death, and the Commander-in-Chief (Lord Combermere) undertook the siege in December 1825, with an army of 21,000 men, and a battering train of 112 pieces.

Lord Lake's disastrous failure in 1805 against this fortress was due to contempt of the enemy, insufficient preparations, a ridiculously small battering train, and an almost entire lack of engineers and equipment.

These faults were sedulously avoided on this occasion, and the fortress taken by assault after an enormous breach had been made by mining.

Troops employed :—

General Lord Combermere, C.-in-C.

Cavalry Division :—Brigadier J. W. Sleigh, 11th Light Dragoons.

1st Brigade :—Brigadier G. H. Murray, 16th Lancers.
  H.M. 16th Lancers.
  6th, 8th, and 9th Bengal L. Cavalry.

2nd Brigade :—Brigadier M. Childers, 11th Light Dragoons.
  H.M. 11th Light Dragoons.
  3rd, 4th, and 10th Bengal L. Cavalry.

Artillery :—Brigadier A. M'Leod.
Bengal Horse Artillery :—Brigadier C. Brown.
1st Brigade :—2nd Troop.
2nd Brigade :—1st, details of 2nd, and 3rd and 4th Troops.
3rd Brigade :—1st, 2nd and 4th Troops.
Bengal Foot Artillery :—Brigadier R. Hetzler.
  1st Battalion :—2nd, 3rd, and 4th Companies.
  3rd Battalion :—1st, 2nd, and 4th Companies.
  4th Battalion :—2nd and 3rd Companies.

Bengal Engineers :—Brigadier T. Anburey.
  6 Companies of Sappers and Miners, and 2 Companies of Pioneers.

1st Infantry Division :—Major-General T. Reynell.
1st Brigade :—Brigadier J. M'Combe, 14th Foot.
    H.M. 14th Foot.
    23rd and 63rd Bengal N.I.
4th Brigade :—Brigadier T. Whitehead, 41st B.N.I
    32nd, 41st, and 58th Bengal N.I.
5th Brigade :—Brigadier R. Paton, 18th B.N.I.
    6th, 18th, and 60th Bengal N.I.
2nd Infantry Division :—Major-General J. Nicolls.
2nd Brigade :—Brigadier G. McGregor, 59th Foot, succeeded by
        Brigadier W. T. Edwards, 14th Foot, who was
        killed in the assault.
    H.M. 59th Foot.
    11th and 31st Bengal N.I.
3rd Brigade :—Brigadier J. W. Adams, 4th Extra B.N.I.
    33rd, 36th, and 37th Bengal N.I.
6th Brigade :—Brigadier W. T. Edwards, 14th Foot, succeeded by
        Brigadier C. S. Fagan, 15th B.N.I.
    15th, 21st, and 35th Bengal N.I.

In addition the following troops were present :—
Two corps of Irregular Horse, Lieut.-Colonel J. Skinner, viz.,
the 1st and 8th Local Horse ; detachments from 1st Nusseeree and
Sirmoor Battalions ; one wing 1st Bengal European Regt., which
arrived on 9th January, 1826, and detachment of the 3rd Extra N.I.
The siege train, 112 pieces, arrived on 14th and 15th December.

Assault on 18th January, 1826.

Right Column :—Lieut.-Colonel J. Delamain, 58th B.N.I.
    2 Cos. Ben. Eur. Regt.
    58th B.N.I.
    100 Gurkhas, 1st Nusseeree Battn.

Main Right Column :—Major-General T. Reynell.
Brigadier R. Paton ..
    4 Cos. H.M. 14th Foot.
    5 Cos. 41st B.N.I.
    6th B.N.I.
Brigadier J. M'Combe ..
    4 Cos. H.M. 14th Foot.
    23rd and 60th B.N.I.
Reserve (Brig. T. Whitehead)..
    2 Cos. H.M. 14th Foot.
    18th and 32nd B.N.I.

Main Left Column :—Major-General J. Nicolls.
Brigadier W. T. Edwards (killed)
    H.M. 59th Foot.
    31st, 15th, and 21st B.N.I.
Reserve (Brig. J. W. Adams) .. 36th and 37th B.N.I.

Intermediate Column.

Lieut.-Colonel T. Wilson, 33rd B.N.I.

{ 2 Cos. Bengal European Regt.
Grenadier Co., 35th B.N.I.
Light Co., 37th B.N.I.
100 Ghurkhas, Sirmoor Battalion. }

Casualties at the assault :—

Europeans .. 81 killed. 303 wounded. 2 missing.
Natives .. 42 ,, 189 ,, 9 ,,

Total casualties during the siege :—

180 killed, 780 wounded, 20 missing.

Twelve British and one Native officer, present at this siege, had taken part in Lord Lake's unsuccessful siege in 1805.

The prize money amounted to nearly £500,000 sterling, of which the Commander-in-Chief's share was nearly £60,000, a lieutenant's nearly £250, a sergeant's £8, a private's £4, and a Sepoy's £2 14s.

Three British artillerymen deserted to the enemy during the siege ; and one of them who had served at Waterloo in the Royal Artillery was hanged on the N.E. Bastion after the capture of the fortress ; the two others were transported.

Engineers (Bengal Presidency) engaged.

Lieut.-Colonel T. Anburey, c.b., Brigadier.
Capt. R. Smith (wounded).
,, J. Taylor (wounded).
,, J. Colvin (wounded).
,, C. J. C. Davidson.
Lieut. W. N. Forbes (wounded).
,, A. Irvine, Brigade-Major (wounded).
,, E. Swetenham.
,, E. J. Smith (wounded).
,, H. de Bude (wounded).
,, J. Thomson.
,, J. Tindall (killed).
,, B. Y. Reilly.
,, G. T. Greene.
2nd Lieut. H. Goodwyn.
,, A. H. E. Boileau.

AFGHANISTAN, 1839–42.

Medal for Ghuznee, 1839.

1·5-in. diameter, silver.

Obverse.—The gateway of Ghuznee, " GHUZNEE."

Reverse.—A mural crown within a laurel wreath, and the date, " 23ᴰ July 1839 "

Ribbon.—Yellow and green, or crimson and green in equal halves, 1¼ in. wide.

Mounting.—A straight silver bar, pivoted.

The First Afghan War, 1839–42.

Practically none of the medal rolls for this campaign are extant, either in England or in India, but it is possible by means of collateral official documents to verify nearly all the medals issued to the Queen's troops, and a fair proportion of those issued to Europeans in the Company's service.

The exact number of medals struck for the capture of Ghuznee, 23rd July, 1839, is not known, but the total number of men entitled to it, including the Bengal, Bombay and Shah Shujah's troops was about 11,700. They were issued at first unengraved, but in 1844 the Court of Directors gave instructions that arrangements should be made in future for engraving all medals before issue ; and as will be seen later this was done with practically all the medals granted for the 1842 campaign, with the exception of the first Jellalabad medals.

From various records it is evident that very great delay occurred in issuing the Ghuznee 1839 medals to the troops in the Company's service, if not to the Queen's troops, and it is probable that a number were issued officially engraved. The medals were not struck till toward the end of 1842.

No papers are extant showing the particulars of the change of the ribbon from yellow and green to crimson and green ; but the reason was (in all probability) to introduce the colours of the ribbon of the Star of the Durani Empire, an order constituted by Shah Shujah after his reinstatement by the British. Sir T. Willshire's medal with the original yellow and green ribbon is to be seen in the museum of the Royal United Service Institution, Whitehall ; but owing to the delay in issuing the medal it is improbable that this ribbon was extensively worn.

The design of the medal was settled by a committee of officers, and it is pretty certain that the obverse depicting the Cabul gate of the fortress, which was blown in, is taken from a drawing executed by Lieut. H. M. Durand, of the Bengal Engineers, the officer who blew in the gate.

Several European firms were invited to submit dies and proofs to the Calcutta Mint, the cost being defrayed by the Government, and it is not at all unlikely that the Ghuznee medals met with occasionally, which differ slightly from the authorized design, are faked proofs from the rejected dies. The striking of the medals from the approved dies was done at the Calcutta Mint, and the dies are still in custody there.

The invasion of Afghanistan was undertaken for the purpose of dethroning Dost Mahomed, and reinstating the exiled Shah Shujah. The Army of the Indus was composed of two corps under the command of Sir H. Fane, C.-in-C. in India. The Bengal column concentrated at Ferozepore in December, 1838, and was to form a junction with the Bombay column, under Sir John Keane, on the Indus.

The raising of the Siege of Herat led to a reduction of the invading army, the 3rd Infantry Brigade of the Bengal column was left at Ferozepore, and Sir H. Fane relinquished the command to Sir J. Keane.

The Indus was crossed at Bhakkar, which fortress was taken possession of, and the army commenced its painful march through the Bolan Pass to Quetta. The losses in baggage, transport and followers from marauders were enormous, the troops were half starved, and the immense army of followers almost entirely so, as they were put on quarter rations. At Quetta the 2nd Infantry Brigade (Major-General W. Nott) was left in garrison and the march resumed to Candahar.

The 37th B.N.I., a detachment of Shah Shujah's force, and all the battering train were left at this latter place, as it was understood that Ghuznee, which lay between the army and its objective, Cabul, was an insignificant fort.

On arrival at Ghuznee, the C.-in-C. found to his dismay a formidable fortress. The Chief Engineer gave his opinion that the proper course was to mask the fortress and continue the march on Cabul. Sir J. Keane made the disconcerting answer that this course was impossible as the army had provisions for *two days only*. Capt. Thomson thereupon stated that the only course open was to attempt to seize the fortress by a *coup de main*.

Making a very careful reconnaissance on the 21st July, he ascertained that the Cabul gate was the only one which had not been built up, and he laid before the General a scheme for blowing this gate open and seizing the fortress by assault. The General approved the plan (none other was possible), which was to be carried into execution at 3 a.m. on 23rd July. Cavalry and artillery were posted in suitable positions while the storming column made its desperate venture.

The advance explosion party consisted of Capt. A. C. Peat, Bombay Engineers ; Lieut. H. M. Durand, Bengal Engineers ; Lieut. N. C. Macleod, Bengal Engineers ; and 3 sergeants, and 18 sappers carrying 300 lbs. of powder, with 6 men of the 13th L.I. Their escort consisted of 300 men of the 13th L.I. who extended and kept up a fire on the parapets.

Then came the advance party of the light companies of the 2nd Foot, 17th Foot, and Bengal European Regiments and one company 13th L.I., guided by Lieut. J. L. D. Sturt, Bengal Engineers, and commanded by Colonel Dennie, of the 13th L.I.

Next followed the storming column, guided by Capt. Thomson, the Chief Engineer, and commanded by Brigadier Sale, consisting of the remainder of the 2nd, 13th, 17th and Bengal European Regiments ;

D

while lastly there was a native reserve under Brigadier Roberts composed of the 16th, 35th and 48th Bengal N.I. The whole of the European infantry of the army was thus thrown into the storming column.

Durand laid and fired the charge, and he himself has told the story of how nearly the whole scheme failed through the chances of night operations and stray casualties. Fortunately the " almost " failure turned into a " complete " success, and Ghuznee fell.

The fall of Ghuznee was a staggering blow to Dost Mahomed. Cabul was occupied without opposition, Shah Shujah was installed on the throne, and after some desultory fighting Dost Mahomed surrendered himself and was deported to India.

GHUZNEE.
Investment, 21st July ; Assault, 23rd July, 1839.

Troops present on these dates, and entitled to the medal :—
Lieut.-General Sir J. Keane, Commander-in-Chief.
Major-General J. Thackwell, Commanding Cavalry Division.

Bengal Column.—Major-General Sir W. Cotton.
Cavalry :—Brigadier R. Arnold, 16th Lancers.
        H.M. 16th Lancers.
        2nd Bengal Light Cavalry.
        3rd Bengal Light Cavalry.
        4th Local Horse (Skinner's), detachment.
Artillery :—Lieut.-Colonel P. L. Pew.
        2-2nd Brigade Bengal Horse Artillery.
        2-6th Battalion Bengal Foot Artillery.
Engineers :—Capt. G. Thomson, Chief Engineer.
        2nd and 3rd Cos., Bengal Sappers and Miners.
Infantry :—
    1st Brigade :—Brigadier R. H. Sale, 13th Foot.
        H.M. 13th Foot.
        16th B.N.I. and 48th B.N.I.
    4th Brigade :—Brigadier A. Roberts,* European Regiment.
        1st Bengal European Regiment.
        35th B.N.I.

Bombay Column.—Major-General T. Willshire.
Cavalry :—Brigadier J. Scott, 4th Light Dragoons.
        H.M. 4th Light Dragoons (2 squadrons).
        1st Bombay Light Cavalry.
        Poona Horse (detachment 300 strong).
Artillery :—Brigadier T. Stevenson (in chief command)
        3rd and 4th Troops Bombay Horse Artillery.
        2-2nd Battn. Bombay Foot Artillery.
        1st Co. Golundaz Battalion.
        * Father of F.M. Lord Roberts.

PLATE III.

EARLY INDIAN CAMPAIGNS AND THE DECORATIONS
AWARDED FOR THEM.

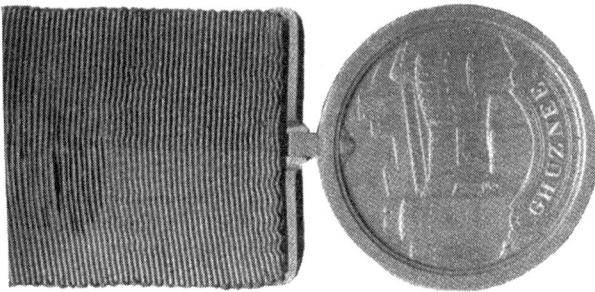

GHUZNEE. 1839.

PLATE IV.

EARLY INDIAN CAMPAIGNS AND THE DECORATIONS
AWARDED FOR THEM.

JELLALABAD. 1842.

(First Medal).

Engineers :—Capt. A. C. Peat.
Infantry :—Brigadier J. G. Baumgardt, 2nd Queen's.
        H.M. 2nd Queen's Regiment.
        H.M. 17th Foot.
        19th Bombay N.I.

Note.—The 2nd Bengal Light Cavalry was disbanded for cowardice at Parwandara, 2nd November, 1840.

The 2nd Infantry Brigade (Major-General W. Nott), consisting of the 31st, 42nd, and 43rd Bengal N.I., had been left at Quetta and elsewhere.

The 3rd Infantry Brigade never advanced beyond Ferozepore.

The 37th Bengal N.I. from the 4th Brigade was left at Candahar with the 4-2nd Battn. Bengal Artillery ; and other units and details not mentioned here were left behind at Quetta, in Scinde or elsewhere.

Casualties.—The total casualties on the 21st and 23rd July amounted to 18 men killed, 20 British officers and 153 other ranks wounded, 2 men missing.

A large portion of Shah Shujah's Force under the command of Major-General E. H. Simpson was present also and received the medal.

This force was raised in India, officered by British officers (assisted by a sprinkling of British N. C. officers), and paid by the Indian Government ; it was intended to form the nucleus of the Shah's future army.

On 23rd July, 1839, the British *personnel* and units of the force were as follows :—

Shah Shujah's Force, 23. 7. 1839.

Major-General E. H. Simpson, 19th B.N.I., Commanding.
Capt. J. Griffin, 24th B.N.I., A.D.C.
Capt. T. McSherry, 30th B.N.I., Brigade-Major.

Horse Artillery	Capt. W. Anderson, Ben. Art.
	Lieut. G. L. Cooper, ,, ,,
	Lieut. F. Turner, ,, ,,
1st Cavalry	Capt. J. Christie, 3rd Ben. L. C.
2nd Cavalry	Lieut. W. Anderson, 59th B.N.I.
	Lieut. D. Gaussen, 42nd B.N.I.
1st Infantry	Capt. J. D. D. Bean, 23rd B.N.I.
	Lieut. P. Nicholson, 28th B.N.I.
	Sergt.-Major W. Mathews.
2nd Infantry	Capt. C. G. Macan, 16th B.N.I.
	Lieut. J. Hoppe, 16th B.N.I.
	Sergt.-Major T. Smith.
3rd Infantry	Capt. J. H. Craigie, 20th B.N.I.
	Lieut. R. McKean, 17th B.N.I.
	Sergt.-Major N. McDoudd.

4th Infantry (Ghoorkas)	Capt. I. H. Handscomb, 26th B.N.I.
	Lieut. T. E. Moorhouse, 35th B.N.I.
	Sergt.-Major R. Young.
5th Infantry	Capt. J. Woodburne, 44th B.N.I.
	Lieut. J. K. Spense, 20th B.N.I.
	Sergt.-Major W. Fitch.
Commissariat Agent	Capt. H. Johnson, 26th B.N.I.
Medical Establishment	Surgeon J. Forsyth, Ben. Med. Est.
	Asst. Surgeon G. Rae.
	,, ,, C. Mackinnon.
	,, ,, H. Baddeley.

The force was increased to a total strength of

      2 troops Horse Artillery.
      Mountain Train.
      A corps of Shah's Own Artillery.
      A battalion of Sappers & Miners.
      2 regiments of Cavalry.
      6 battalions of Infantry.

The British *personnel* of officers and N.C. officers was increased also. The fate of the contingent was as follows :—

The 4th Infantry was destroyed at Charikar in November, 1841, particulars of which are given below.

The 6th Infantry was destroyed in the retreat from Cabul, together with half the corps of Sappers & Miners, half the Mountain Train, and the small corps of Shah's Own Artillery.

The 3rd Infantry was taken on to the strength of the Bengal Army.

The 5th Troop, 1st Brigade, Bengal Horse Artillery, was formed from the Shah's Horse Artillery, and the 7th and 8th Companies, Bengal Sappers & Miners, from the remnants of the Shah's Sappers & Miners in 1842. The remaining corps were disbanded.

The commanding officers of the force at the end of 1841 were as follows :—

      Brigadier T. J. Anquetil, Commanding.
      Horse Artillery.—Capt. W. Anderson.
      1st Cavalry.—Capt. J. Christie.
      2nd Cavalry.—Capt. W. Anderson.
      Mountain Train.—Capt. J. B. Backhouse.
      Shah's Own Artillery.—Lieut. R. Warburton.
      Sappers & Miners.—Capt. G. Broadfoot.
      1st Infantry.—Capt. J. Griffin.
      2nd Infantry.—Capt. C. G. Macan.
      3rd Infantry.—Capt. J. H. Craigie.
      4th Infantry.—Capt. C. Codrington.
      5th Infantry.—Capt. J. Woodburne.
      6th Infantry.—Capt. P. Hopkins.

No medal was given for the assault and capture of Khelat (Baluchistan) on 13th November, 1839, although it is borne as a distinction on the colours of the regiments engaged; and occasionally an unofficial bar engraved " Khelat " is found on a Ghuznee medal.

The troops detached for this service (under the command of Major-General T. Willshire) were :—

> 2 guns 3rd Troop, Bombay Horse Artillery.
> 4 guns 1st Troop, Shah's Horse Artillery.
> Detachment Bombay Engineers & Sappers.
> 2 rissalas 4th Local Horse (Skinner's).
> H.M. 2nd and 17th Foot (343 and 400 strong).
> 31st Bengal N.I.

Casualties.—31 killed and 107 wounded.

After the surrender of Dost Mahomed the Army of Occupation was largely reduced, the returning corps marching back to India through the Khyber Pass which had now been opened. The remaining garrison was scattered throughout Afghanistan, at Candahar, Khelat-i-Ghilzie, Ghuznee, Cabul, and Charikar.

Continual desultory fighting had continued throughout 1840-1, but the garrison was being further reduced by the marching of Sale's brigade from Cabul toward India, when the storm burst in October, 1841, sweeping away the garrisons of Cabul, Charikar and Ghuznee, and driving Sale's brigade to take refuge in Jellalabad. In Southern Afghanistan Khelat-i-Ghilzie held out, and at Candahar Nott kept the field the whole winter, though all communications with India were cut.

The story of the unfortunate results of the first attempts to relieve Jellalabad by Brigadier Wild, and to reinforce Nott at Candahar by Major-General England is well known, as also the later successful efforts by Pollock and England respectively. Jellalabad was relieved by Pollock on 16th April, 1842, nine days after the famous sortie of 7th April, and England reached Candahar on the 10th May. After three months of indecision the Government of India approved Pollock's plans for an advance on Cabul and for Nott's " retirement " to India *via* Cabul and the Khyber Pass. The subsequent operations of both Generals were entirely successful ; and it only remains to enumerate the various corps who took part in the first disasters and subsequent successes.

Troops Destroyed at Charikar, November, 1841.

The 4th Shah's (Ghoorka) Infantry, under Capt. C. Codrington, and a detachment of the Shah's Own Artillery.

Only the Political Officer (Major E. Pottinger), one officer of the 4th Shah's Infantry (Ensign J. C. Haughton) and one Ghoorka, succeeded in escaping to Cabul ; one or two other natives escaped independently and 165 Ghoorkas were rescued in 1842 by Haughton, after Pollock's advance to Cabul.

Troops Destroyed near Cabul, January, 1842, under Major-General W. G. K. Elphinstone.

The numbers given below are the approximate strengths of the corps on commencing the retreat from Cabul, 6th January, 1842.

1-1st Brigade Bengal Horse Artillery (90 men, 6 guns), Capt. T. Nicholl.

Half Shah's Mountain Train (3 guns, 30 men), Lieut. C. A. Greene, Bengal Artillery.

Shah's Own Artillery, Lieut. R. Warburton,* Bengal Artillery.

Half Shah's Sappers (240 men), Lieut. W. Bird, 30th Mad. N.I.

Detachment Bengal Sappers & Miners (20 men) attached to the A.Q.M.G.

2nd Shah's Cavalry (500 men), Capt. W. Anderson, 59th B.N.I.

5th Bengal L. Cavalry (260 men), Lieut.-Colonel R. E. Chambers.

Det. 1st Irregular Cavalry
Det. 4th Irregular Cavalry } Skinner's Horse (140 men).

The late Envoy's Escort (70 sabres).

H.M. 44th Foot (600 men), Major W. B. Scott.

5th Bengal N.I. (700 men), Major S. Swayne.

37th   ,,   ,,   (600 men), Major C. Griffiths.

54th   ,,   ,,   (650 men), Major W. Ewart.

6th Shah's Infantry (600 men), Capt. P. Hopkins, 27th B.N.I., and details of other corps.

Colonel J. Shelton, 44th Foot, was acting as Brigadier, and Brigadier T. J. Anquetil commanded Shah Shujah's force.

The casualties during the three months preceding the retreat had been very heavy ; 101 British officers were killed in and near Cabul between 12th October, 1841, and 14th January, 1842.

Major-General Elphinstone died in captivity.

N.B.—Pollock recovered in September, 1842, 34 British officers, 12 ladies, 22 children, 1 warrant officer, 7 men of the 13th Foot, 38 men of the 44th Foot, 6 Europeans of the Bengal Horse Artillery, 2 European clerks, and many hundreds of Sepoys and followers.

Troops Destroyed at Ghuznee, March, 1842.

27th Bengal N.I., Lieut.-Colonel T. Palmer.

Six British officers of this regiment (including the future hero, John Nicholson) were recovered by Pollock, and 327 Sepoys by Nott in September near Ghuznee.

From the above it may be seen that the popular statements of the British losses are greatly exaggerated. The total number of the troops (British and Native) destroyed in Afghanistan during this period may be reckoned at 900 Europeans and 4,500 Natives at the

* Father of Colonel Sir R. Warburton, K.C.I.E., Political Officer, Khyber Pass, 1879—1897.

outside, of whom nearly all the Europeans and 3,600 Sepoys were killed at Cabul and in the retreat towards Jellalabad. These numbers do not, of course, include the followers of the army, large numbers of whom perished or were taken prisoners and sold into slavery.

JELLALABAD.

Defence under Sir R. Sale, 12th November, 1841, to 16th April, 1842 :—

Garrison :—

> H.M. 13th Foot.
> 5th Bengal Light Cavalry (1 squadron).
> 2nd Shah's Cavalry (1 rissala).
> 2-6th Battn. Bengal Artillery.
> Two men of the 1-1st Brigade Bengal Horse Artillery.
> Half the Shah's Mountain Train.
> Half the Shah's Sappers (Broadfoot's).
> 35th Bengal N.I.
> Detachment 6th Shah's Infantry (doing duty with Mountain Train).
> Sergt.-Major of 37th B.N.I. (who escaped from Cabul), and details.
> Followers—682 armed, 630 unarmed.

Casualties, 22nd February, 1842, to 7th April, 1842 :—

> 1 British officer and 35 men killed.
> 7 „ officers and 141 other ranks wounded.

Four guns were recaptured in the sortie of the 7th April.

For their gallantry during the war in Ava, 1824–6, and in the defence of Jellalabad, the 13th Foot were given the title of " Prince Albert's " Light Infantry, and their facings changed from yellow to blue.

A large number of the Native officers of the 35th B.N.I. were recommended for the Orders of Merit, and British India for their gallantry.

Jellalabad.—Medals were issued to the surviving members of the garrison on December 14th, 1842, prior to their triumphal entry into Ferozepore. All these medals were unnamed. The dies are at the Calcutta Mint and are now cracked. An " unofficial " die has been made by some unknown person ; but the difference can be easily detected.

In his order dated 17th December, 1842, Lord Ellenborough stated that medals would be sent in due course to the relatives of soldiers of the garrison who had deceased on or after April 7th, 1842 ; and as in his letter to the Court of Directors dated 19th October, 1842, he had asked for a new medal to be struck, it is almost certain that the relatives of deceased soldiers received the second or " Flying

Victory " medal, as it is called. A considerably larger number of " Flying Victory " medals were issued than is generally supposed.

Medals seem to have been struck off and impressed for most of the officers of the garrison, although some never applied to have their original medals exchanged. The 13th Foot sailed from India for England in December, 1844, leaving behind 446 men who had exchanged into other regiments serving in the country. Some time after their arrival home a return was sent in giving the names of those men still in the regiment who had not *yet* exchanged their medals. This list comprises nearly 200 men, and medals were struck and impressed for all of them, mounted with the China 1842 suspender. About 50 of these men are noted as having exchanged their medals *after* the date of this return, and 139 were sold to a Mr. Nash in 1860 by the India Office.

Many men of the 13th Foot wore the 2nd Jellalabad medal with a parti-coloured crimson and blue ribbon, but the authority for this is not known.

The actual number of men entitled to receive the Jellalabad medal was 2,596. The exact distribution of this number is not available, but the following is a very close approximation :—

H.M. 13th Foot	780
5th Bengal L. Cavalry	160
2nd Shah's Cavalry	100
2-6th Battn. Bengal Artillery	150
Shah's Mountain Train	65
Shah's Sappers (Broadfoot's)	400
35th Bengal N. Infantry	900
Details	41

A few " Flying Victory " medals exist with the obverse of the China 1842 medal, bearing the legend " Victoria Regina " instead of " Victoria Vindex." It can be stated *definitely* from the examination of records that in some cases such medals were late re-issues, and it is probable that all were ; and this remark applies to the few similar medals given for Cabul, Candahar, etc.

With regard to the " Candahar " medal it is to be noted that the dies are kept in India. This fact seems to have been unknown at the Royal Mint, for to meet the demand for two re-issues in later years (one an officer's and the other a private's medal) two medals were struck from the " Candahar, Ghuznee, Cabul " die, and the words " Ghuznee, Cabul," erased. I am not aware that either of these medals have been met with by collectors. No other re-issues of " Candahar " medals appear to have been made in England.

At least two dies were used for the " Candahar " medals, as minute differences can be seen by a careful observer.

CABUL, 1842.

Troops that formed " The Avenging Army " under Major-General G. Pollock's Command.

Cavalry :—Brigadier M. White, 3rd L. Dragoons.
    H.M. 3rd Light Dragoons.
    1st and 10th Bengal Light Cavalry.
    3rd (Tait's) Irregular Cavalry.

Artillery :—Major H. Delafosse, Bengal Artillery.
    3-1st Brigade and 3-2nd Brigade Bengal Horse Artillery.
    2-2nd Battn. and 4-6th Battn. Bengal Artillery.
    Mountain Train (2 guns).
    " E " Co. Syce Drivers.

Engineers :—Capt. F. Abbott, Bengal Engineers, Chief Engineer.
    5th Co. Bengal Sappers & Miners.
    A corps of Pioneers (Lieut. F. Mackeson).

Infantry Division :—Major-General J. McCaskill, 9th Foot.
  *2nd Brigade :—Brigadier J. Tulloch.
    H.M. 9th Foot.
    26th and 60th Bengal N.I.
    5th Co. Bengal Sappers & Miners.

  3rd Brigade :—Brigadier C. F. Wild.
    30th, 53rd, 64th Bengal N.I.

  4th Brigade :—Brigadier T. Monteath, 35th B.N.I.
    H.M. 31st Foot.
    6th and 33rd Bengal N.I.

A Sikh contingent with Capt. H. M. Lawrence,† Ben. Art., and Capt. J. Ferris' Afghan Jezailchis co-operated.

N.B.—(a). The Brigadier of the 4th Brigade was commanding his regiment, 35th N.I., in Jellalabad. (b). The 31st Foot arrived a good deal later than the 9th Foot, and did not share in the forcing of the Khyber Pass and Relief of Jellalabad in April. (c). Only the 3rd Company of the 6th B.N.I. received the medal ; while of the 33rd B.N.I. only two companies were at the forcing of the Khyber Pass and Relief of Jellalabad.

After the Relief of Jellalabad on 16th April, the garrison was amalgamated with Pollock's force, and H.M. 13th Foot, the 35th B.N.I., Broadfoot's Sappers, and the Khyber Rangers (Capt. H. P. Burn, 1st B.N.I.) formed the 1st Brigade under Sir R. Sale's command.

    ° For 1st Brigade see below.
    † Later Sir Henry Lawrence, K.C.B., killed at Lucknow.

The only unit of the Jellalabad garrison that did not advance with Pollock (other than details) was the remnant of the 2nd Shah's Cavalry. This corps did not receive the Cabul medal ; nor was it granted to the friendly Afghan levies that accompanied Pollock, or to Mackeson's semi-civil corps of pioneers : only the British officers of these corps received the medal.

Troops at CANDAHAR, *January*, 1842, *under Major-General W. Nott.*

1st (Bengal) Irregular Cavalry (Skinner's).
1st Shah's Cavalry.
1st and 2nd Troops Shah's Horse Artillery.
Half 4-2nd Battn. Bengal Artillery.
3-1st Battn. Bombay Artillery.
H.M. 40th Foot.
2nd, 16th, 38th, 42nd, and 43rd (six companies only) Bengal N.I.
1st, 2nd, and 5th Shah's Infantry.

Garrison of KHELAT-I-GHILZIE, *under Capt. J. H. Craigie, 3rd Shah's Infantry.*

Half 4-2nd Battn. Bengal Artillery.
Det. Bengal Sappers and Miners (from the 2nd and 3rd Companies).
3 companies 43rd Bengal N.I.
3rd Shah's Infantry.

Nott relieved the garrison of Khelat-i-Ghilzie on May 26th and brought it back to Candahar.

Reinforcements from INDIA, *under Major-General R. England, which arrived at Candahar on* 10th May, 1842.

1st Troop Bombay Horse Artillery.
3-2nd Battn. Bengal Artillery.
Half C Co., Madras Sappers and Miners.
3rd Bombay Light Cavalry.
Poona Irregular Horse (one rissala).
H.M. 41st Foot.
25th Bombay N.I.
Bombay L. Infantry Battalion (probably formed from the light companies of the battalions stationed in Upper Scinde, viz. :—6th, 8th, 20th, 21st and 25th Bombay N.I.).

N.B.—105 men of H.M. 41st Foot and details did not arrive at Candahar till 27th June, 1842.

*Troops that returned to India, via Quetta, under Major-General R.
England, on 10th August, 1842.*

1st Troop Shah's Horse Artillery.
Half the 4-2nd Battn. Bengal Artillery.
1st Shah's Cavalry (2 rissalas).
Poona Irregular Horse (1 rissala).
1st, 2nd, and 5th Shah's Infantry.
25th Bombay N.I.
Bombay Light Infantry Battn.
Sick and details of other corps.

Troops that Marched from CANDAHAR *on* GHUZNEE *and* CABUL,
with Major-General W. Nott, 10th August, 1842.

Artillery :—Major F. S. Sotheby, Ben. Art., Commanding.
1st Troop Bombay Horse Artillery.
2nd Troop Shah's Horse Artillery.
3-2nd Battn. Bengal Artillery.
Det. 4-2nd Battn. Bengal Artillery doing duty with the
3-2nd Battalion.
3-1st Battn. Bombay Artillery.

Engineers :—Major E. Sanders, Bengal Engineers, Chief Engineer.
Det. Bengal Sappers & Miners (from the 2nd and 3rd Cos.).
Half C Co., Madras Sappers & Miners.

Cavalry :—Capt. C. H. Delamain, 3rd Bombay Light Cavalry,
Commanding.
1st (Bengal) Irregular Cavalry.
3rd Bombay Light Cavalry.
1st Shah's Cavalry (less 2 rissalas).

Infantry :—

1st Brigade :—Brigadier G. P. Wymer, 38th B.N.I.
H.M. 40th Foot.
16th and 38th Bengal N.I.
3rd Shah's Infantry.

2nd Brigade :—Brigadier L. R. Stacy, 43rd B.N.I.
H.M. 41st Foot.
2nd, 42nd, 43rd Bengal N.I.

N.B.—In the cavalry action at Oosman-Khan-ki-karez, on 28th
August, 1842, the Subadar-Major of the 3rd Bombay L. Cavalry,
" who wore the medal for Seringapatam," was killed.

On his march from Candahar to Cabul, Nott captured ten guns, and recovered 327 men of the 27th Bengal N.I., many of whom did duty with other corps thenceforward.

The casualties in action sustained by Nott's force, between 1st January, 1842, and the 17th September, the date of his arrival at Cabul, were some 70 killed (including 3 British officers) and 330 wounded.

For their gallantry in this campaign the 2nd and 16th Bengal N.I. were made Grenadiers, and the 38th, 42nd and 43rd Bengal N.I. were constituted Light Infantry.

For their share in the defence of Khelat-i-Ghilzie the 3rd Shah's Infantry was brought on to the strength of the Bengal Army as " The Regiment of Khelat-i-Ghilzie," and still exists as the 12th Khelat-i-Ghilzie Regiment.

Jellalabad, 1842.—First Medal.

1·5-in. diameter, silver.

Obverse.—A mural crown, " JELLALABAD."

Reverse.—The date " VII. April 1842."

Mounting.—A straight silver brooch with a loop in the centre engaging a small silver ring from which the medal is suspended.

N.B.—This original mounting, being rather weak, is not often seen.

Second Medal.

1·4-in. diameter, silver.

Obverse.—Crowned head of Queen Victoria.
 Legend " Victoria Vindex."

Reverse.—Victory flying over the fort of Jellalabad.
 Inscription, " JELLALABAD VII April MDCCCXLII."

Mounting.—German silver bar, secured to the medal by two concealed pins.

N.B.—This also is a weak mounting, and not often seen.

Khelat-i-Ghilzie, 1842.

1·4-in. diameter, silver.

Obverse.—A shield inscribed " KHELAT-I-GHILZIE," surrounded by a laurel wreath, and surmounted by a crown.

Reverse.—A military trophy, " INVICTA MDCCCXLII."

Mounting.—A steel bar and clip.

Candahar, Ghuznee, Cabul, 1842.

Four medals, 1·4-in. diameter, silver.

Obverse.—As for the 2nd Jellalabad medal.

Reverse.—(a). " CANDAHAR 1842 " within a wreath, surmounted
by a crown.

(b). " CABUL 1842 " within a wreath, surmounted by
a crown.

(c). " CANDAHAR GHUZNEE CABUL 1842 " within a
wreath surmounted by a crown.

(d). " GHUZNEE " " CABUL " each within a wreath :
a crown above ; " 1842 " below.

Mounting.—Steel bar and clip.

The ribbon for all these medals, including the Jellalabad and
Khelat-i-Ghilzie medals, is the military ribbon of India, 1¾ in. wide.
This ribbon was designed by Lord Ellenborough for the Jellalabad
medal, crimson shading into yellow, and yellow into blue. It was
intended to be the " military " ribbon of India, just as the crimson
ribbon with blue edges was the " military " ribbon of Great Britain ;
and as such was worn with the Scinde and Gwalior medals of 1843.
It was revived as the ribbon for the bronze star granted for the march
from Cabul to Candahar, 1880, but in a narrower width. Many men
of the 13th Foot wore a parti-coloured crimson and blue ribbon with
the *second* Jellalabad medal, but the authority for this is not known.*

Khelat-i-Ghilzie.

932 medals in all were struck, as follows :—

Staff and details	.. ..	7
4-2nd Battn. Bengal Artillery	86	(of whom 1 officer and 43 men were Europeans).
Bengal Sappers and Miners ..	23	(Details from Nos. 2 and 3 Companies).
43rd Bengal N. Infantry ..	247	(3 companies).
3rd Shah's Infantry	569	

With few exceptions most of the above received the " Ghuznee-
Cabul " medal as well.

* The original ribbon issued to the Jellalabad garrison was made in
Coventry of 1¼-in. width only. The parti-coloured crimson and blue
ribbon was probably introduced into the 13th L.I. under regimental
authority, as a distinguishing ribbon which showed the colour of their
new facings.

The following list gives the number of medals struck for Major-General Nott's force :—

	Candahar, Ghuznee, Cabul.	Ghuznee, Cabul.	Candahar.
Staff and details	23	3	5
H.M. 40th Foot	669	3	64
H.M. 41st Foot	494	105	26
1st Troop, Bombay H. Artillery	—	138	—
3-1st Battn. Bombay Artillery	91	25	2
3-2nd Battn. Bengal Artillery..	17	87	1
4-2nd Battn. Bengal Artillery..	10	38	28
1st Troop, Shah's H. Artillery	—	—	127
2nd Troop, Shah's H. Artillery	121	—	1
Bengal Sappers and Miners (details 2nd and 3rd Cos.) ..	3	24	—
Madras Sappers & Miners, C Co.	1	28	—
3rd Bombay Light Cavalry ..	—	354	—
1st Bengal Irregular Cavalry ..	282	17	17
1st Shah's Cavalry	469	1	198
2nd Bengal N.I.	893	4	65
16th ,, ,, ...	795	4	31
38th ,, ,, ...	854	5	107
42nd ,, ,, ...	852	1	79
43rd ,, ,, ...	637	169	37
1st Shah's Infantry	—	—	640
2nd ,, ,, ...	—	—	592
3rd ,, ,, ...	—	521	—
5th ,, ,, ...	—	—	595
Totals	6,211	1,527	2,615

It is to be noted that this list does not include the " Candahar " medals to which detachments from the Poona Irregular Horse, 25th Bombay N.I. and the Bombay Light Infantry Battalion were entitled. The omission seems to have been accidental, owing to their not having come under Nott's direct personal command, and correspondence ensued on this subject. The actual number of " Candahar " medals issued to them later on is not discoverable, but the claim was allowed.

A " Candahar " medal was issued later on to Sir R. England, who scarcely came within the terms of Lord Ellenborough's order of 4th October, 1842, authorizing the medal ; and his first application for it seems to have been rejected.

Of the 64 " Candahar " medals struck for the 40th Foot, 42 were for the relatives of deceased officers and soldiers, and 22 for sick, etc., who returned to India from " Candahar " viâ Quetta. In the same way most of the " Candahar " medals struck for the 41st Foot were for the relatives of deceased soldiers.

The 105 men of that regiment who received the " Ghuznee-Cabul " medal arrived in Candahar late in June, some seven weeks after the main body : as also did the two officers and one man (three in all) of the 40th Foot who received the " Ghuznee-Cabul " medal. The late Field Marshal Sir N. B. Chamberlain and his brother, General Sir C. T. Chamberlain, served as subalterns with the 1st Shah's Cavalry, one brother receiving the " Candahar-Ghuznee-Cabul " medal, and the other that for " Candahar."

The distribution of the " Cabul " medals struck is given below :—

Staff, etc.	38
3-1st Brigade Bengal H. Artillery	129
3-2nd ,, ,, ,,	139
2-2nd Battn. Bengal Artillery	97
2-6th ,, ,, ,,	123
4-6th ,, ,, ,,	109
Mountain Train	56
E Company Syce Drivers	153
H.M. 3rd Light Dragoons	489
1st Bengal Light Cavalry	453
5th ,, ,, ,,	142
10th ,, ,, ,,	498
3rd (Tait's) Irregular Cavalry	739
H.M. 9th Foot	831
H.M. 13th Foot	745
H.M. 31st Foot	826
6th Bengal N.I. (3rd Co. only)	112
26th ,, ,,	1,004
30th ,, ,,	920
33rd ,, ,,	947
35th ,, ,,	837
53rd ,, ,,	915
60th ,, ,,	1,012
64th ,, ,,	927
5th Company, Bengal Sappers and Miners	125
Shah's Sappers (Broadfoot's)	375
Total	12,741

The numbers of medals struck (especially " Candahar " medals) may surprise a good many collectors, but the comparative rarity is to be gauged by the number of *European* recipients, which may be estimated approximately as follows :—

Khelat-i-Ghilzie	55
Candahar	130
Ghuznee-Cabul	360
Jellalabad	800
Candahar—Ghuznee—Cabul	1,400
Cabul	3,500

All the medals for this campaign (except the 1st Jellalabad medals) were engraved before issue, with the exception of many of those given to the Shah's troops, and *many officers' medals*.

The total number of medals was therefore approximately 27,000, viz. :—

Jellalabad	2,596
Khelat-i-Ghilzie	932
Cabul	12,741
Candahar	2,615
Ghuznee, Cabul	1,527
Candahar, Ghuznee, Cabul ..	6,211

Total .. 26,622, exclusive of some later claims.

The amount of ribbon ordered was 14,000 yards, from which it appears that half a yard was issued with each medal.

There are few medals that repay careful study in a greater degree than those given for this campaign or to which so much interest is attached.

Engineer Officers who served in Afghanistan, 1839–42.

(*a*). 1839.

G. Capt. G. B. Thomson, Bengal Engineers, Chief Engineer.
G. Lieut. J. Anderson, Bengal Engineers, Surveyor.
G.   ,,   H. M. Durand, Bengal Engineers, Surveyor.
—   ,,   J. Laughton, Bengal Engineers, Field Engineer (left at Bhakkur as Garrison Engineer).
— Capt. E. Sanders, Bengal Engineers, Sappers and Miners (sent from Candahar on mission to Herat).
G. Lieut. J. L. D. Sturt, Bengal Engineers, Sappers & Miners.
G.   ,,   N. C. Macleod, Bengal Engineers, Sappers & Miners.
G.   ,,   R. Pigou, Bengal Engineers, Sappers & Miners.
G.   ,,   J. S. Broadfoot, Bengal Engineers, Sappers & Miners.
G.K. Capt. A. C. Peat, Bombay Engineers (wounded).
— Lieut. C. F. North, Bombay Engineers, Field Engineer (to Herat with Sanders).
G. Lieut. W. F. Marriott, Bombay Engineers, Field Engineer (wounded).
G.K. Lieut. F. Wemyss (Senior), Bombay Sappers & Miners.
—   ,,   J. D. Cunningham, Bengal Engineers, Political Assistant with Colonel C. M. Wade (to Cabul *viâ* Khyber Pass in 1839).

G. denotes presence at the Storm of Ghuznee, 23rd July, 1839.
K. denotes presence at the Storm of Khelat, 13th November, 1839.

PLATE V.

EARLY INDIAN CAMPAIGNS AND THE DECORATIONS AWARDED FOR THEM.

JELLALABAD. 1842.
(Second Medal).

KHELAT-I-GHILZIE. 1842.

PLATE VI.

EARLY INDIAN CAMPAIGNS AND THE DECORATIONS
AWARDED FOR THEM.

AFGHANISTAN. 1842.
(Obverse as in Plate V.).

(b). 1840–42. (Killed in Action).

Lieut. J. S. Broadfoot, Bengal Engineers, killed at Parwandara, 2. 11. 40.

,, R. Pigou, Bengal Engineers, killed by explosion at fort gate in Nazian Valley, 24. 2. 41.

,, J. L. D. Sturt, Bengal Engineers, killed in retreat from Cabul, 9. 1. 42.

(c). Defence of Khelat-i-Ghilzie, 1842.

Lieut. (Major) R. Leech, Bombay Engineers, Political Officer.

,, T. Studdert, Bombay Engineers, Executive Engineer.

(d). With Major-General Nott, " Candahar, Ghuznee, and Cabul, 1842."

Major E. Sanders, Bengal Engineers, Chief Engineer (wounded, April, 1841).

Lieut. C. F. North, Bengal Engineers.

,, (Major) R. Leech, Bombay Engineers, Political Officer.

,, T. Studdert, Bombay Engineers.

(e). With Major-General Pollock, " Cabul, 1842."

Capt. F. Abbott, Bengal Engineers, Chief Engineer.

Lieut. J. W. Robertson, Bengal Engineers.

,, A. G. Goodwyn, ,, ,,

,, J. R. Becher, ,, ,,

,, J. S. Alexander, Bengal Engineers (wounded), with Brigadier Wild at the first attempt to relieve Jellalabad (with Pollock later (?)).

N.B.—Officers who served in Scinde are not included above.

The utter rashness of the Afghan War was demonstrated still more plainly in the years immediately following, for the British were involved in hostilities with the powerful states of Scinde, Gwalior, and the Punjab in rapid succession ; and it was through these territories that the lines of communication of the army in Afghanistan ran.

SCINDE CAMPAIGN, 1843.

The relations of the British with the Amirs of Scinde had not been very happy since the opening of the Afghan War in 1839 ; and the unsatisfactory state of affairs culminated in a treacherous attack on the British Residency at Hyderabad on 15th February, 1843. The escort of the Resident (Major James Outram) consisted of the light company of H.M. 22nd Foot, and in the river there were lying close by the two small steamers *Planet* and *Satellite*, and a flat. Outram withdrew his men on to these vessels without much

E

difficulty, and joined Sir C. J. Napier who was on the alert at Halla 35 miles north-west of Hyderabad, and was already marching to attack the enemy.

On the 17th February he came into contact with them on the banks of the Fulaili Nullah at Meeanee, 6 miles from Hyderabad, and after a desperate fight against a foe five times as numerous as his own force, defeated them with immense slaughter. His small force did not permit of much tactics; he advanced in echelon across the flat ground, and as the troops closed on the enemy, the Baluchis made successive charges at close quarters, but were slowly driven from the field with the loss of all their guns, etc. Hyderabad was entered on the 20th February and Scinde annexed on 12th March; but one Sirdar, Mir Sher Mohammed, still remained in the field with 20,000 men at Dubba, some 4 miles from Hyderabad.

Having been reinforced Napier marched to the attack, and found the Baluchis (as before) posted behind a nullah.

A preliminary shelling from the artillery, followed by an advance of the infantry, compelled the enemy to give ground; and the turning of both flanks by the cavalry turned the retreat into an utter rout.

Troops engaged at Meeanee, 17th February, 1843.

9th Bengal Light Cavalry.
Scinde Irregular Horse.
Poona Irregular Horse* (detachment).
2-2nd Battn. Bombay Artillery.
3rd Company Golundaz, Bombay Artillery.
Madras Sappers and Miners (half C Company).
H.M. 22nd Foot.
1st Bombay Grenadiers.
12th and 25th* Bombay N.I.

Casualties :— 6 officers and 56 other ranks killed.
13   ,,   181   ,, ,,   wounded.

Troops engaged at Hyderabad, 24th March, 1843.

The corps at Meeanee, as above.
1st Troop Bombay Horse Artillery.†
2-1st Battn. Bombay Artillery.
Remainder of C Company Madras Sappers.†
3rd Bombay Light Cavalry.†
8th and 21st Bombay N.I.

Casualties :— 2 officers and 37 other ranks killed.
10   ,,   221 ,,   ,,   wounded.

* Recently with England in Afghanistan.
† Recently with Nott in Afghanistan.

Garrison of Entrenched Camp at Dubba, 24th March, 1843.

Detachment 6th Bombay N.I.
15th Bombay N.I.
Details from corps in the field.

At the attack on the Residency, 15th February, 1843, the Resident's escort (viz. the Light Company of H.M. 22nd Foot) and a naval force of some 110 men were engaged, on H.C.V. *Planet, Satellite* and a flat.

The casualties were insignificant, but the naval detachment received the Meeanee medal for the affair, although none of them were present at the battle two days later.

In the same way the crews of the H.C.V. *Comet, Meteor* and *Nimrod* (115 men in all) received the medal for Hyderabad, although stationed in the Indus, off Dubba, several miles away.

It is extremely doubtful if the 15th Bombay N.I. and those details from the 6th Bombay N.I. and other corps which garrisoned the entrenched camp at Dubba, received the medal, although actually nearer the field of battle than the Indus Flotilla.

The total number of Meeanee medals struck is much greater than is usually supposed, being as under :—

H.M. 22nd Foot	65
Artillery	63
Sappers	14
9th Bengal Cavalry	?*
Scinde Irregular Horse	90
Poona Irregular Horse	14
1st Bombay Grenadiers	148
12th Bombay N.I.	153
25th Bombay N.I.	206
Miscellaneous	8
Indus Flotilla (Naval)	110

Here again the comparative rarity of the medal must be gauged by the number of European recipients, which (including officers) was some 120, of whom 40 were naval.

The European Naval medals for Hyderabad numbered 60.

All the *Naval* medals for this campaign seem to have been issued with the " China, 1842," suspender, and were impressed.

The medals issued to the Company's troops (European and Native) are often indented on the rim (apparently in India) ; while others and those of the 22nd Foot have block engraving.

* Returns not available (say 90).

Scinde, 1843.

Three medals, 1·4-in. diameter, silver.

Obverse.—Crowned head of Queen Victoria.

> Legend " Victoria Regina."

Reverse.—(*a*). " MEEANEE 1843 " within a wreath, surmounted by a crown.

> (*b*). " HYDERABAD 1843 " within a wreath, surmounted by a crown.

> (*c*). " MEEANEE HYDERABAD 1843 " within a wreath, surmounted by a crown.

Mounting.—Steel bar and clip for non-commissioned ranks; silver ditto for officers.

Ribbon.—Military ribbon of India, 1¾ in. wide.

N.B.—The steel bars and clips of the medals issued to the 22nd Foot were replaced by silver ones, by Colonel Pennefather ; and this was also done very generally by other corps, European and Native.

Engineer Officers employed in the Campaign.

M.H. *Lieut. E. J. Brown, Ben. Engrs., Secretary to the Resident.

M.H. Capt. R. Henderson, Mad. Engrs.   } C Company, Madras

M.H. Lieut. A. J. M. Boileau, Mad. Engrs. } Sappers & Miners.

M.H. Major C. Waddington, Bo. Engrs.

H. Lieut. T. Studdert, Bo. Engrs.

— Lieut. C. A. Orr, Mad. Engrs. (did not receive a medal).

> M. signifies present at the Battle of Meeanee.
> H. signifies present at the Battle of Hyderabad.

GWALIOR, 1843.

This campaign was occasioned by the disturbances which followed on the death of the Maharajah. To overawe the disputants the Governor-General (Lord Ellenborough) mobilized at Agra and Jhansi an " Army of Exercise" under Sir H. Gough, the Commander-in-Chief.

The peace manœuvres however changed so rapidly to operations of war that the Governor-General, and four ladies who had come to look on, came under fire from the Mahratta guns.

The two wings of the " Army of Gwalior " fought battles independently of each other at Maharajpore and Punniar respectively on the same day, 29th December, 1843.

The British losses at Maharajpore were very heavy, as the infantry made a frontal attack on an entrenched position held by an enemy with a powerful artillery.

* Present also at attack on Residency, 15th February, 1843.

PLATE VII.

EARLY INDIAN CAMPAIGNS AND THE DECORATIONS
AWARDED FOR THEM.

SCINDE. 1843.

PLATE VIII.

EARLY INDIAN CAMPAIGNS AND THE DECORATIONS
AWARDED FOR THEM.

GWALIOR.   1843.

At Punniar matters were managed better. An attack by the British on the centre and left of the Mahratta position was completely successful at slight cost.

For both these battles bronze stars with silver insets were given, and Lord Ellenborough gave the four ladies present at Maharajpore gold and enamel stars of a special pattern, bearing the Queen's head.

For the succeeding operations in 1844, in the southern Mahratta country, no medal was given, nor for the operations on the Scinde Frontier which were of a most arduous nature, and which lasted till 1845.

Gwalior, 1843.

Two medals. A six-pointed bronze star, with silver inset.

Reverse.—Quite plain.

Obverse.—(a). " MAHARAJPOOR 29th Decr 1843."
  (b). " PUNNIAR 29th Decr 1843."

Mounting.—A bronze hook at the back.

N.B.—The stars were made from the captured guns. Later on most recipients added mountings of varied designs, and wore the medal with the " Military Ribbon of India."

The medals as originally designed had a silver elephant in the centre ; but, on account of the expense of manufacture, a star was substituted ; and it is believed that Lord Gough was the only soldier to receive and wear the bronze star of the original design.

As in the case of the 1st Afghan War, no medal rolls for this campaign are available either in India or England, but in the case of the Queen's troops it is possible to verify their medals in most instances from other official documents, and sometimes those of Europeans in the H.E.I.C.S. The engraving on the backs of the stars is very typical and shows readily whether a medal is worth paying attention to.

Troops present at Maharajpore, 29th December, 1843.

Right Wing, Army of Gwalior, Lieut.-General Sir H. Gough, C.-in-C.
  Cavalry :—Major-General Sir J. Thackwell.

  3rd Brigade :—Brigadier C. R. Cureton, 16th Lancers.
  H.M. 16th Lancers.
  1st Bengal Light Cavalry.
  4th Irregular Cavalry (in reserve).

  4th Brigade :—Brigadier J. Scott, 9th Lancers.
  The Governor-General's Bodyguard.
  4th and 10th Bengal Light Cavalry.

2nd Infantry Division :—Brigadier J. Dennis, 3rd Foot.
    3rd Brigade :—Brigadier T. Valiant, 40th Foot.
        H.M. 40th Foot.
        2nd and 16th Bengal N.I.
    4th Brigade :—Brigadier L. R. Stacy, 43rd B.N.I.
        14th, 31st, and 43rd Bengal N.I.
3rd Infantry Division :—Major-General J. H. Littler.
    5th Brigade :—Brigadier T. Wright, 39th Foot.
        H.M. 39th Foot.
        56th Bengal N.I.*
    6th Brigade (in reserve) :—Brigadier S. D. Riley, 62nd B.N.I.
        62nd and 70th Bengal N.I. (not engaged).
        Khelat-i-Ghilzie Regiment (only flank companies engaged).

Detachments of the 5th and 8th Bengal L. Cavalry, and one company 39th B.N.I. were also present, probably as escorts.

Artillery :—Brigadier G. E. Gowan.

Bengal Horse Artillery :—2nd and 3rd Troops, 2nd Brigade.
                     2nd Troop, 3rd Brigade.
Bengal Foot Artillery :—1st Company 1st Battalion.
                     1st Company 4th Battalion.
                     2nd, 3rd, 4th Companies 4th Battalion
                     (in reserve), also Native Reserve of
                     5th, 8th, 9th and 10th Companies
                     6th Battalion.

Engineers :—Major E. J. Smith.

3rd, 4th, 7th Companies Bengal Sappers and Miners.

Casualties :— 5 British officers and 101 other ranks killed.
           34   ,,   ,,   654   ,,   wounded.
56 guns were captured. Among the killed was Major-General C. H. Churchill, C.B., Q.M.G., Queen's Troops, a Waterloo veteran.

Troops present at Punniar, 29th December, 1843.

Left Wing, Army of Gwalior, Major-General J. Grey in command.
  1st Cavalry Brigade :—Brigadier A. Campbell, 9th Lancers.
      2 squadrons H.M. 9th Lancers.
      5th and 11th Bengal L. Cavalry (2 squadrons each).
  2nd Cavalry Brigade :—Brigadier D. Harriott, 8th L. Cavalry.
      8th Bengal L. Cavalry.
      8th Irregular Cavalry.
      Cavalry, Bundelkhand Legion.

---

* The 3rd Battalion of this brigade, viz., the 35th B.N.I., was left at Agra.

1st Infantry Brigade :—Brigadier W. A. Yates, 51st B.N.I.
    H. M. 3rd Buffs.
    39th and 51st Bengal N.I.
    Bundelkhand Legion.
2nd Infantry Brigade :—Brigadier J. Anderson, 50th Foot.
    H.M. 50th Foot.
    50th and 58th Bengal N.I.
Artillery :—Brigadier E. Biddulph.
    Bengal Horse Artillery :—1st and 3rd Troops, 3rd Brigade.
    Bengal Foot Artillery :—6th Company 6th Battalion.
Engineers :—
    1st Company Bengal Sappers and Miners.
Sipri Contingent :—Brigadier O. Stubbs, 24th B.N.I.
Casualties :—2 British officers and   35 other ranks killed.
           7   ,,   ,,   175   ,,   wounded.
24 guns were captured.

Officers of the Bengal Engineers present at Maharajpore.

Major E. J. Smith, Chief Engineer.
  ,,   E. Sanders, Deputy Secretary to Government of India,
        Military Department (killed).
Capt. H. M. Durand, Private Secretary to Governor-General.
Lieut. W. Abercrombie, Brigade-Major.
  ,,   T. Renny-Tailyour, Quartermaster.
  ,,   C. B. Young.
  ,,   S. Pott.
  ,,   D. Campbell.
  ,,   W. D. A. R. Shortt.
  ,,   J. E. T. Nicolls.

Officer of Bengal Engineers present at Punniar.

Lieut. J. H. Maxwell.

    N.B.—This list is perhaps incomplete.

THE SUTLEJ CAMPAIGN, 1845–6.

The anarchy that ensued soon after the death of Runjeet Singh
in 1839, culminated in the Sikh Army crossing the Sutlej and invading
British territory in December, 1845. The Governor-General (Sir H.
Hardinge), who was touring on the frontier at the time, immediately
issued orders for the concentration of the British troops under Sir
H. Gough, the C.-in-C., and marched with them himself.

    Ten days after leaving their cantonments, and in which they covered
150 miles, the advanced portion of the British Army came into
contact at Moodkee, on 18th December, with a detached corps of the

Sikhs, thrown out in front of their main army and entrenched camp at Ferozeshah.

The battle began with artillery fire, while the British infantry advanced in echelon of brigades and deployed.   Meanwhile the small force of British cavalry was directed to turn *both* flanks of the vastly superior force of the Sikhs.   Both charges were executed with the greatest gallantry and success, and the infantry, advancing in echelon of lines, drove back the enemy with the bayonet, until night and weariness put an end to the battle.

Great confusion prevailed during the battle, the infantry had come into action, after a long march through deep sand, with stragglers stretching out for miles in rear ; a dust storm was blowing, and many casualties were caused (as in other battles of this war) by the Native regiments, which lagged behind, firing into the European regiments in front.

The Sikhs lost some 17 guns and fell back on their main army at Ferozeshah.

The next day, H.M. 29th Foot, the 1st Bengal Europeans, and other troops arrived, and the Governor-General tendered his military services to Sir H. Gough, as second-in-command.

On the 21st December the army resumed its march, but, by the personal order of the Governor-General, the Commander-in-Chief was forbidden to commence the attack on the Ferozeshah entrenchments until (as arranged) Sir John Littler, who had slipped out of Ferozepore, leaving a small garrison to oppose Sirdar Tej Singh, had effected a junction.

This took place early in the afternoon, and the assault on one of the longer faces of the camp then took place.   Sir John Littler's division was on the extreme left.   Sir H. Hardinge commanded the left wing of Gough's force and Gough commanded the right wing on the right flank.

The Sikhs numbered 47,000 men with 88 guns, according to their own estimate, the British numbered 17,000 men with 69 guns.

Littler's division assaulted the trenches prematurely and unsupported, and was driven back with immense loss ; meanwhile the 2nd and 3rd Divisions attacked and penetrated the entrenchments, but could not clear the camp ; the 1st Division (in reserve) also succeeded in penetrating the entrenchments.   Night had now ensued, all the regiments and brigades were hopelessly mixed up and scattered, and the Sikhs kept up fire during a great part of the night.

In the morning Sir H. Hardinge and Sir H. Gough re-formed such troops as were at hand, and leading the line in person, 20 paces ahead, to prevent premature firing, swept the camp from end to end, driving the Sikhs from the field and capturing 74 guns.

Scarcely had this been effected, when Sirdar Tej Singh with 35,000 men and 100 guns arrived from Ferozepore.

The situation of the British was critical in the extreme ; nearly all the artillery ammunition had been fired away, and the troops were worn out. The men were, however, immediately formed up and preparations for attack made, when Tej Singh, bluffed by the British, and doubly cautious after learning how the main army of the Sikhs had been turned out of their entrenchments, withdrew.

The British losses totalled 2,877 ; and, as before, the European regiments had to do most of the fighting. Sir H. Hardinge, who had served throughout the Peninsular War, considered the Bengal Native regiments much on a par with Portuguese troops, and that like them they had their fighting days. Unfortunately the 21st December was one of their non-fighting days.

The Sikhs now took up a position at Sobraon, with the Sutlej and their bridge of boats immediately in their rear, and spent their time entrenching themselves again. The chance of giving them a knock-out blow in this position was recognized by Sir H. Hardinge, and they were left there unmolested, pending the arrival of reinforcements and a siege train.

Meanwhile a Sikh Sirdar crossed the Sutlej higher up, threatening Ludhiana and the British communications. Sir H. Smith was detached to deal with him, which he did most effectively at the Battle of Aliwal on 28th January, 1846. Each arm was given full scope, the infantry advanced in line, covered by artillery fire, with cavalry on either flank. The enemy's left was turned and their line crumpled up and taken in reverse. The Sikh right, composed of Avitabile's crack battalions, clung to their ground to cover the passage of the Sutlej in rear, until H.M. 16th Lancers broke their square and the whole army was driven pell-mell across the river with the loss of every gun (67 in all), and at least 3,000 men.

The only point east of the Sutlej now held by the Sikhs was their bridgehead at Sobraon, and as soon as the siege train and reserve ammunition arrived, Sir H. Gough and Sir H. Hardinge planned the assault.

The Sikh entrenchments were held by 35,000 troops (exclusive of irregular cavalry), with 70 guns, while 50 pieces of heavy artillery were posted on the right bank. The British force *engaged* numbered 16,000 men. The engagement began by a heavy cannonading, but the infantry attack had to be launched prematurely owing to the expenditure of gun ammunition—one of the chief defects revealed by the campaign being the shortage of gun ammunition carried in the field by the artillery.

The 3rd Division, on the left, first penetrated the entrenchments, followed soon after by the 2nd and 1st Divisions on the centre and right. For an hour the battle raged inside the position before the Sikhs were broken, but by midday the enemy had been driven across the river ; during their passage the bridge broke, and the river, which had risen several inches during the night, swept the Sikhs. away by hundreds, while the horse artillery played upon them un-- ceasingly from the river's edge. No less than 10,000 Sikhs perished that day, the position and sandbanks in the river were thickly piled with corpses, and 67 of their guns remained in our possession.

The British crossed the Sutlej the same day, and on the 20th February arrived at Lahore. Under the terms of the treaty of peace the remainder of their heavy guns, used in action, had to be surrendered.

The war occupied almost exactly two calendar months, during which four big battles were fought, over 200 pieces of artillery captured on the field, and nearly 7,000 casualties sustained in action, of which the few British regiments suffered no less than 3,600, out of a total strength of a little more than 9,000 of all ranks.

Sir H. Hardinge authorized, in the first instance, the medals for this war ; and, following the rule followed in the Peninsula, directed that medals should be given for the battles only, the name of the first battle in which the recipient was engaged being on the reverse of the medal, while those of subsequent battles were on clasps attached to it.

Sutlej Campaign, 1845-6.

Obverse.—Crowned head of Queen Victoria. Legend : " Victoria Regina."

Reverse.—Victory standing beside a trophy, holding a wreath in her outstretched hand. Inscription: "Army of the Sutlej."

Exergue.—(a) " Moodkee 1845.
       (b) " Ferozeshuhur 1845."
       (c) " Aliwal 1846."
       (d) " Sobraon 1846."

Clasps.—" Ferozeshuhur."
      " Aliwal."
      " Sobraon."

Mounting.—Silver scroll bar and swivel. This was the first medal issued with a swivel mounting.

Ribbon.—Dark blue with crimson edges, 1¼ in. wide.

N.B.—The correct name of the village that gave its name to the battle of Ferozeshuhur, is " Ferushahr." This battle honour is spelt officially as " Ferozeshah."

SUTLEJ CAMPAIGN, 1845-6 (Sir H. Gough, C.-in-C.).

Troops present at Moodkee, 18th December, 1845.

Cavalry :—Brigadier M. White, 3rd L. Dragoons.
     2nd Brigade :—Brigadier J. B. Gough, 3rd L. Dragoons (wounded at Sobraon).
       H.M. 3rd Light Dragoons.
       The Bodyguard.
       5th Bengal Light Cavalry.

3rd Brigade :—Brigadier W. Mactier, 4th L.C. (wounded).
   4th Bengal Light Cavalry.
   9th Irregular Cavalry.
Artillery :—Brigadier G. Brooke.
Horse Artillery :—1st Brigade, 1st, 2nd, and 3rd Troops.
        3rd Brigade, 1st, 4th and 1 division of 2nd Troop.
Foot Artillery :—3-4th Battn. and 2-6th Battn.
Engineers :—Major R. Napier.*
Infantry :—
   1st Division :—Major-General Sir H. G. Smith.
      1st Brigade :—Brigadier S. Bolton, 31st Foot (killed).
      H.M. 31st Foot.
      24th and 47th Bengal N.I.
      2nd Brigade :—Brigadier H. M. Wheeler,† 48th B.N.I.
         (wounded).
      H.M. 50th Foot.
      42nd and 48th Bengal N.I.
   2nd Division :—Major-General W. R. Gilbert, 38th N.I.
      2nd, 16th, and 45th Bengal N.I.
      (Remainder of Division not yet arrived).
   3rd Division :—Major-General Sir J. M'Caskill, 9th Foot (killed).
      Brigadier N. Wallace, 26th B.N.I.
      H.M. 9th and 80th Foot.
      26th and 73rd Bengal N.I.
      (Remainder of Division not yet arrived).
Casualties :—12 British officers and 203 other ranks killed.
     44   ,,   ,,   613   ,,   ,,   wounded.
17 or 19 guns were taken, exact number is uncertain.
Sir R. Sale, of Jellalabad fame, was among the killed.
On the 19th December H.M. 26th Foot, the 1st Bengal European
Regt., 11th and 41st Bengal N.I., the 2-4th Battn. and 4-4th Battn.
Bengal Artillery arrived.
The 11th and 41st B.N.I. were left at Moodkee to guard the
wounded, and the army marched on the 21st to effect a junction with
Littler's division from Ferozepore.
Sir J. H. Littler left in garrison at Ferozepore the 27th and 63rd
B.N.I., the 2-2nd Battn. Bengal Artillery, 3 guns of 2-7th Battn.
Bengal Artillery and a detachment of Bengal Sappers ; and marched
with the 8th Bengal Light Cavalry and the 3rd Irregular Cavalry,
5-1st Brigade and 3-3rd Brigade Bengal Horse Artillery, 4-6th
Battn., 3 guns 2-7th Battn. and detail of 2-2nd Battn. Bengal Artillery,
detachment of Bengal Sappers, the 7th Infantry Brigade (H.M. 62nd
Foot, 12th and 14th B.N.I.) and 8th Infantry Brigade (33rd, 44th
and 54th Bengal N.I.).

* Later F.M. Lord Napier of Magdala.
† Killed at Cawnpore, 1857.

Troops present at Ferozeshah, 21st, 22nd December, 1845.

Cavalry :—Brigadier D. Harriott, 8th Ben. L.C. (wounded).

 1st Brigade :—Brigadier M. White, 3rd L. Dragoons (wounded)
  H.M. 3rd Light Dragoons.
  4th Bengal Light Cavalry.
  9th Irregular Cavalry.

 2nd Brigade :—Brigadier J. B. Gough, 3rd L. Dragoons.
  The Bodyguard.
  5th Bengal Light Cavalry.

 3rd Brigade :—Brigadier D. Harriott (commanding the
  Division).
  8th Bengal Light Cavalry.
  3rd Irregular Cavalry.

Bengal Horse Artillery :—Brigadier G. Brooke.
Bengal Foot Artillery :—Brigadier G. G. Dennis.

  1st Brigade H.A. :—1st, 2nd, 3rd and 5th Troops.
  3rd Brigade H.A. :—1st, 3rd, 4th, and 1 division of 2nd
   Troops.
  4th Battn. :—2nd, 3rd and 4th Cos.
  6th Battn. :—2nd and 4th Cos.
  7th Battn. :—3 guns of 2nd Co.
  Also detail of 2-2nd Battn.

Bengal Engineers :—Major R. Napier.
 No. 6 Co., Sappers and Miners.

1st Infantry Division :—Major-General Sir H. G. Smith.

 1st Brigade :—Brigadier G. Hicks, 47th B.N.I.
  H.M. 31st Foot.
  24th and 47th B.N.I.

 2nd Brigade :—Brigadier T. Ryan, 50th Foot.
  H.M. 50th Foot.
  42nd and 48th B.N.I.

2nd Division :—Major-General W. R. Gilbert.

 3rd Brigade :—Brigadier C. C. Taylor, 29th Foot (wounded).
  H.M. 29th and 80th Foot.
  45th B.N.I.

 4th Brigade :—Brigadier J. McLaren, 16th B.N.I.
  1st Bengal European Regiment.
  2nd and 16th B.N.I.

3rd Division :—Brigadier N. Wallace, 26th B.N.I. (killed).

 5th Brigade :—H.M. 9th Foot.
   26th and 73rd B.N.I.
 6th Brigade :—Absent.

4th Division :—Major-General Sir J. H. Littler, 36th B.N.I.
    7th Brigade :—Brigadier T. Reid, 62nd Foot (wounded).
        H.M. 62nd Foot.
        12th and 14th B.N.I.
    8th Brigade :—Brigadier T. Ashburnham, 62nd Foot.
        33rd, 44th, and 54th B.N.I.

Casualties :—39 British officers and   681 other ranks killed.
        82   ,,   ,,   1,686   ,,   ,, wounded.
                             379   ,,   ,, missing.
74 guns were captured.

It is to be noted that the troops that guarded the camp at Moodkee, and those that garrisoned Ferozepore, received the decoration for Ferozeshah.

Troops present at Aliwal, 28th January, 1846 (Sir H. G. Smith in command).

Cavalry Division :—Brigadier C. R. Cureton, 16th Lancers.
    1st Brigade :—Brigadier G. J. M. McDowell, 16th Lancers.
        H.M. 16th Lancers.
        3rd Bengal Light Cavalry.
        4th Irregular Cavalry.
    2nd Brigade :—Brigadier R. A. Stedman, 1st Bengal L. Cavalry.
        The Bodyguard.
        1st and 5th Bengal L. Cavalry.
Bengal Artillery :—Major G. S. Lawrenson.
Horse Artillery :—1-1st Brigade, 1st and 3rd Troops, 2nd Brigade, 2-3rd Brigade.
Foot Artillery :—2-7th Battn.
Bengal Engineers :
    Detachment, Sappers and Miners.
Infantry :—
    1st Brigade :—Brigadier G. Hicks, 47th B.N.I.
        H.M. 31st Foot.
        47th B.N.I.
    2nd Brigade :—Brigadier H. M. Wheeler, 48th B.N.I.
        (Brigadier N. Penny, Supernumerary).
        H.M. 50th Foot.
        48th B.N.I.
        Sirmoor Battn.
    A Brigade :—Brigadier R. W. Wilson, 30th B.N.I.
        H.M. 53rd Foot.
        30th B.N.I.
        (Wing 24th B.N.I., probably in garrison at Ludhiana).

A Brigade :—Brigadier C. Godby, 36th B.N.I.
    36th B.N.I.
    Nusseeree Battn.
    Bengal Sappers and Miners.
Shekawati Brigade :—Major H. Foster.
    Cavalry, Artillery, and Infantry, 1,200 strong.
Casualties :— 4 British officers and 147 other ranks killed.
    25   ,,   ,,   388   ,, ,, wounded.
                   25   ,, ,, missing.
67 guns captured or destroyed.

N.B.—A good many details and drafts of other corps were present by accident, and the decoration was given to the garrisons of Ludhiana and Buddhowal Forts.

These included detachments from 2-4th, 4-4th, and 4-6th Battns. Bengal Artillery, Wing 24th B.N.I., etc.

Troops present at the Battle of Sobraon, 10th February, 1846 (Sir H. Gough, C.-in-C.).

Cavalry Division :—Major-General Sir J. Thackwell.
    1st Brigade :—Brigadier J. Scott, 9th Lancers.
        H.M. 3rd Light Dragoons.
        8th and 9th Irregular Cavalry.
    2nd Brigade :—Brigadier A. Campbell, 9th Lancers.
        H.M. 9th Lancers.
        2nd Irregular Cavalry.
    3rd Brigade (on the right of the army, near Hurreekee Ford) :—
        Brigadier C. R. Cureton, 15th Lancers.
        H.M. 16th Lancers.
        The Bodyguard.
        3rd, 4th and 5th Bengal Light Cavalry.
Bengal Artillery :—Brigadier G. E. Gowan.
1st Division Horse Artillery :—Brigadier G. Brooke.
2nd Division Horse Artillery :—Brigadier E. Biddulph.
    1st Brigade Horse Artillery, 2nd, 3rd and 5th Troops.
    2nd   ,,   ,,   ,,   1st, 2nd and 3rd Troops.
    3rd   ,,   ,,   ,,   1st, 2nd, 3rd and 4th Troops.
Foot Artillery :—Brigadier G. G. Dennis.
    2-2nd Battn. ; 3rd and 4th Cos., 3rd Battn. ; 1st, 2nd, 3rd and 4th Cos., 4th Battn. ; 1st, 2nd, 3rd and 4th Cos., 6th Battn.
Bengal Engineers :—[Brigadier A. Irvine]*.
        Brigadier E. J. Smith.
    Headquarters and 6 Cos. Sappers and Miners.

* Brigadier Irvine waived his right to supersede Smith, as he arrived in camp only just before 10th February.

1st Infantry Division :—Major-General Sir H. G. Smith.
  1st Brigade :—Brigadier N. Penny, Nusseeree Battn. (wounded).
      H.M. 31st Foot.
      47th Bengal N.I.
  2nd Brigade :—Brigadier G. Hicks, 47th Bengal N.I.
      H.M. 50th Foot.
      42nd Bengal N.I.
      Nusseeree Battn.

2nd Infantry Division :—Major-General W. R. Gilbert (wounded).
  3rd Brigade :—Brigadier C. C. Taylor, 29th Foot (killed).
      H.M. 29th Foot.
      41st and 68th Bengal N.I.
  4th Brigade :—Brigadier J. McLaren, 16th Bengal N.I. (killed).
      1st Bengal European Regt.
      16th Bengal N.I.
      Sirmoor Battn.

3rd Infantry Division :—Major-General Sir R. Dick (killed).*
  5th Brigade :—Brigadier Hon. T. Ashburnham, 62nd Foot.
      H.M. 9th and 62nd Foot.
      26th Bengal N.I.
  6th Brigade :—Brigadier C. D. Wilkinson, 63rd Bengal N.I.
      H.M. 80th Foot.
      33rd and 63rd Bengal N.I.
  7th Brigade :—Brigadier L. R. Stacey, 43rd Bengal N.I.
      H.M. 10th and 53rd Foot.
      43rd and 59th Bengal N.I.

Reserve 45th Bengal N.I.
At Rhodawalla, 73rd Bengal N.I.

Also present, wing 24th Bengal N.I., detachment 38th Bengal N.I. and 1 co. 12th Bengal N.I.

Casualties :— 13 British officers and 308 other ranks killed.
            102   ,,   ,,   1,962   ,,   ,, wounded.
67 guns were captured.

The troops at Rhodawalla, and those in reserve, and guarding the Commander-in-Chief's camp received the decoration for Sobraon.

The severity of the casualties in this short campaign of two months, the brunt of which was borne by the European troops, may be gauged from the following :—

  3 Major-Generals and 4 Brigadiers were killed.
  1 Major-General and 7 Brigadiers were wounded.

* Sir R. Dick served with the 42nd Regt. in the Peninsula and at Waterloo.

The European regiments lost 61 officers and 912 men killed, 128
officers and 2,520 men wounded, equivalent to 50 per cent. of the
officers and 40 per cent. of the men.

Strength (approx.) 18. 12. 45.		Corps.	Killed.		Wounded.	
Officers.	Men.		Officers.	Men.	Officers.	Men.
27	518	3rd Light Dragoons ..	6	124	15	142
30	874	9th Foot	4	81	8	267
35	765	29th Foot	4	87	16	331
36	844	31st Foot	9	132	16	352
33	675	50th Foot	8	105	28	445
24	768	62nd Foot	8	91	11	204
26	795	80th Foot	5	63	8	168
26	640	Bengal European Regt. ..	9	80	11	312

Certain of the above regiments received small reinforcing drafts
in January, 1846, which are not included in the strengths given ;
also many individuals were wounded more than once, and increase
the numbers of casualties recorded.

The combination of the Ferozeshah medal with clasps for Aliwal
and Sobraon was not earned by a single individual of the Queen's
troops, and by only a very few in the Company's service.   One or
two well-known collections contain faked medals of British infantry
with this combination.   For practical purposes the combination
may be said to be non-existent.

Medals were issued to the 11th Irregular Cavalry, although this
corps was not really in existence during the war.   The regiment
was ordered to be raised in January, 1846, and a nucleus of British
officers and native ranks, drawn from units serving with the army
in the field, was posted to it on paper.   These individuals served in
the field with their original units, but received their medal later on
as the 11th Irregular Cavalry.   Sir H. G. Smith's despatch written
after the battle at Aliwal mentions a British officer of the " 11th
Irregular Cavalry " who had been posted in orders to that regiment.

Small *Native* detachments of the 4th Irregular Cavalry appear to
have received the decorations for Moodkee and Aliwal.   Faked
clasps of this medal are *very* common ;   *e.g.,* " Aliwal " clasps are
fraudulently added, or " Ferozeshuhur " or " Sobraon " clasps
removed, in order to produce unusual combinations.

Medals were given to Prince Waldemar of Prussia and his suite.
six in all (including two orderlies), who accompanied the Governor-
General in the field as his guests ; one of whom, Dr. Hoffmeister,
was killed at Ferozeshah.

PLATE IX.

EARLY INDIAN CAMPAIGNS AND THE DECORATIONS
AWARDED FOR THEM.

SUTLEJ CAMPAIGN. 1854-6.

Officers of the Bengal Engineers who received medals for the Sutlej Campaign, 1845–6.

S. Lieut.-Colonel A. Irvine.
S.   ,,   ,   E. J. Smith.
S. Major F. Abbott.
S.   ,,   B. Y. Reilly.
S. Capt. W. H. Graham.
S.   ,,   W. E. Baker.
M.F.S.   ,,   R. C. Napier.   (Wounded).   Brigade-Major.
S.   ,,   J. W. Robertson.
S.   ,,   W. Abercrombie.   (Wounded).
S.   ,,   H. Siddons.
A.S. Bt. Capt. J. D. Cunningham.   (Political employ).
S. Lieut. J. Spens.
A.S.   ,,   R. Strachey.
A.S.   ,,   R. Baird Smith.
S.   ,,   A. D. Turnbull.
F.   ,,   A. G. Goodwyn.   (With Littler's force).
S.   ,,   J. R. Becher.   (Wounded).
S.   ,,   H. Yule.
S.   ,,   F. Whiting.
F.A.   ,,   E. J. Lake.   (Wounded).   (Political employ).
S. 2nd Lieut. W. D. A. R. Shortt.
M.   ,,   J. E. T. Nicolls.
A.S.   ,,   G. P. Hebbert.   (Wounded).
S.   ,,   C. J. Hodgson.
S.   ,,   D. G. Robinson.
(F.) A.S.   ,,   A. Taylor.*   (With Littler's force).
S.   ,,   G. Sim.
S.   ,,   C. S. Paton.

M signifies Moodkee.
F   ,,   Ferozeshah.
A   ,,   Aliwal.
S   ,,   Sobraon.

THE PUNJAUB CAMPAIGN, 1848–9.

Exactly two years after the close of the 1st Sikh War hostilities again broke out in April, 1848, on account of the murder at Mooltan of Mr. Vans Agnew and Lieut. Anderson by the Dewan Mulraj.

Lieut. H. B. Edwardes with a force composed almost entirely of irregulars at once took the field, and, defeating Mulraj twice, shut him up in Mooltan.

* Taylor received the decoration for Ferozeshah, as he was on duty in the Ferozepore Cantonment, but he was not present at the battle. In the same way many of the officers with A. or S. before their names were not actually present on the battlefields of Aliwal and Sobraon.

F

Lord Gough had deferred operations purposely until towards the end of the hot weather, when a force was despatched to the siege of Mooltan under Major-General Whish. A Sikh army from Lahore co-operated, but it threw in its lot with the rebel Mulraj on September the 1st.   This compelled Whish to suspend all active offensive operations until he had been reinforced by troops from Bombay and Scinde.   They arrived on December the 21st, the siege was again pressed, and the city taken by assault on January the 2nd.   The citadel held out until January the 22nd, when Mulraj surrendered himself.   Meanwhile the rebellion had spread over the whole Punjaub, and in November the Army of the Punjaub had taken the field under Lord Gough.

The unfortunate cavalry action at Ramnagar (22nd of November) on the left bank of the Chenab was the opening incident of the campaign, in which the 14th Light Dragoons lost their colonel (W. Havelock, brother of Sir H. Havelock), and the cavalry division their general, Brigadier Cureton, the best cavalry officer in India, whose services included the Peninsula War and nearly half-a-dozen wars in India. Among the killed also was the Subadar-Major of the 8th Bengal Light Cavalry—" an old man of 78 years and nearly 60 years' service."

The whole of the army was across the Chenab by December the 8th, and remained inactive till January the 12th, when it moved to attack Sher Singh, who had 30,000 men and 62 guns, near Rasul on the left bank of the Jhelum.

On January the 13th the armies were in contact, but Gough had not intended to fight that day, until it seemed likely that Sher Singh, who had commenced a heavy artillery fire, might take the initiative.

The ground was covered with scrub and jungle, greatly impeding vision and co-ordinated movement.   The Sikh line, which overlapped the British on both flanks, occupied ground slightly higher than the surrounding terrain.   The 2nd Division (Gilbert) was on the right, the 3rd Division (Colin Campbell) on the left, one brigade of which was held in reserve.   On the right flank was the 2nd Cavalry Brigade (Pope), and on the left flank was the 1st Cavalry Brigade (White). The 3rd Brigade (Hearsey) was in reserve.

Before the advance began, Colin Campbell told Brigadier Penny-cuick that, as the scrub made it impossible for him to effectively superintend the advance of the division, he would leave the leading of the 5th Brigade entirely to him, while he himself would accompany the 7th Brigade (Hoggan) which was dangerously outflanked by the Sikhs.

In the advance Gilbert's division was exposed to the greatest danger ; before becoming seriously engaged with the enemy the whole of Pope's cavalry brigade went about, and galloped to the rear,

riding over its own horse artillery and causing the greatest confusion.*
Pope himself was mortally wounded.

Though taken in flank and in rear Gilbert's division pressed on,
repelling all attacks, and carried all before it.

Meanwhile another disaster had befallen the left flank. Penny-
cuick's brigade inclined to its right front, losing touch with the
7th Brigade; and the centre regiment, H.M. 24th Foot, pressing
forward at headlong pace, left the other regiments of the brigade
behind. It arrived quite spent and in disorder at the Sikh batteries,
was unable to withstand a heavy counter-attack, and was driven
back by the Sikh cavalry to a point in rear of that from which it
had started, leaving nearly half its number on the ground.

The 6th Brigade (in reserve) was then pushed into the gap formed.

The 5th Brigade with Colin Campbell had advanced steadily in
the meantime, and captured the batteries in front with great slaughter;
then wheeling to the right it swept along the Sikh position until it
joined hands with the left of Gilbert's division.

The Sikhs were driven from the field, but were not routed, and as
it was now very late in the day it was considered prudent to withdraw
to a more defensible position at Chilianwala. The British casualties
amounted to 2,357. The 24th Foot lost in killed or died of wounds
14 officers and 241 men, and had about 250 more wounded. The Sikh
loss was enormous. " Never except at Sobraon have I seen so many
of the enemy's slain upon the same space," wrote Lord Gough. If
only it had been known how broken the spirit of the Sikhs was, the
British would have encamped on the field that night. As it was,
Sher Singh recrossed the Jhelum in the night, on hearing of the
British retirement, murdered such of the wounded as had been left
behind and recovered most of his guns.

The temper of the British troops did not permit of renewed action
on the morrow and Lord Gough awaited the fall of Mooltan, which
occurred a few days later, when General Whish with all the Bengal
Division, and one strong Bombay brigade, marched to join him. The
last of these troops joined Gough on February the 20th. In the meantime Sher Singh, who had received very numerous reinforcements,
retired and established himself at Goojerat, with 60,000 men and
59 guns.

On February the 15th, Gough marched from Chilianwala, detaching
a force to Wazirabad to prevent any raid across the Chenab on
Lahore.

On February the 21st, the attack on the Sikh position at Goojerat
began with a heavy cannonade which was maintained until the

* It is said that a chaplain in rear was conspicuous in rallying the
fugitives, and that Lord Gough wished to promote him " brevet-bishop"
for his services.

Sikh artillery was overpowered, and their whole line badly shaken. The infantry now advanced, the 1st and 2nd Divisions on the centre of the position, the 3rd Division on the left of the line, and cavalry on both flanks. By one o'clock, after a desperate resistance, the whole Sikh army was in full flight, leaving 56 guns and numberless dead on the field. The pursuit continued for 15 miles that day, and on the morrow Gilbert resumed it with such persistence and relentless vigour that on March the 14th the Sikh chiefs and the remnant of their armies surrendered to him at Rawal Pindi, giving up 41 guns and 20,000 stand of arms. As some allied Afghan cavalry had fought with the Sikhs, Gilbert continued his pursuit to Peshawar, where the remnants of the Afghan cavalry fled through the Khyber Pass.

The whole of the Punjaub was annexed to British India as the result of the war.

The medal for this campaign was authorized in the first instance by Lord Dalhousie, and was given to all troops serving in the Punjaub; the clasp for Chilianwala was granted later at Lord Gough's personal request.

PUNJAUB CAMPAIGN, 1848–9.

Medal 1·4.-in. diameter, silver.

Obverse.—Crowned head of Queen Victoria. Legend " Victoria Regina."

Reverse.—The Sikh army laying down its arms before Sir W. R. Gilbert and his troops near Rawal Pindi. Inscription " To the Army of the Punjab." In exergue " MDCCCXLIX."

Clasps.—" Mooltan."
        " Chilianwala."
        " Goojerat."

Mounting.—Silver scroll bar and swivel.

Ribbon.—Dark blue with two thin yellow stripes, 1¼ in. wide.

Nobody earned the medal with three clasps, but Sir H. M. Lawrence received the medal with two clasps, " Mooltan " and " Chilianwala." He was returning to Lahore from leave in England, and travelling *vià* Karachi and the Indus, spent a few days *en route* at Mooltan, during the last phase of the siege. This combination is, I believe, unique.

The medal with single bar " Mooltan " is not very common to those corps which served at Goojerat as well, *e.g.* the 1-60th Rifles with a strength of nearly 1,000 received less than 100 medals with this one bar, and it is not an uncommon thing to come across a medal to this regiment from which the Goojerat bar has been removed with great care. The irregular levies did not receive any medals.

All the troops quartered in the Punjaub received the medal without the clasp, even if not engaged with the enemy, so that in all some 60,000 medals were issued, with nearly 19,000 clasps for " Mooltan," over 20,000 clasps for " Chilianwala," and about 34,000 clasps for " Goojerat."

The troops who received the medal only were as follows :—

> Bengal Horse Artillery :—2-1st, 3-1st, and 3-3rd Brigade.
> Bengal Foot Artillery :—1-5th, 1-6th, 3-6th, 4-6th, 2-7th, 4-8th and 6-8th Battalion.
> 7th Bengal Cavalry ; 2nd, 13th, 15th, 16th and 17th Irregular Cavalry.
> Bengal Pioneers :—1st Co.
> Bengal Native Infantry:—1st, 3rd, 4th, 18th, 22nd, 29th, 37th, 50th, 53rd, 71st and 73rd N.I.
> Local Corps :—1st and 2nd Regts. Sikh Local Infantry.
> Details of the Indus Flotilla, and of corps in the field.

The troops present at Mooltan, Chilianwala and Goojerat were as follows :—

Troops present at the Siege of Mooltan (18th August, 1848, to 22nd January, 1849. Major-General W. S. Whish, Bengal Artillery, in command).

Bengal Column.

Artillery :—Major H. Garbett.
> 4-1st Brigade and 4-3rd Brigade Horse Artillery.
> 2-2nd Battn., 3rd and 4th Cos., 3rd Battn. and 6-7th Battn. Foot Artillery.

Engineers :—Major R. Napier, succeeded by Brigadier J. Cheape.
> 1st, 2nd and 3rd Cos. Sappers & Miners.
> 2nd and 3rd Cos. and detail of 5th Co. Pioneers.

Cavalry :—Lieut.-Colonel H. F. Salter, 11th Light Cavalry.
> 11th Light Cavalry.
> 7th and 11th Irregular Cavalry.
> Detachment 14th Irregular Cavalry.

1st Infantry Brigade :—Lieut.-Colonel A. Hervey, 52nd N.I.
> H.M. 10th Foot.
> 8th and 52nd Native Infantry.

2nd Infantry Brigade :—Lieut.-Colonel F. Markham, 32nd Foot.
> H.M. 32nd Foot.
> 49th, 51st and 72nd Native Infantry.
> Detachment of the Guides (Lieut. H. B. Lumsden), Sikh contingent under Lieut. H. B. Edwardes, and Bahawalpur contingent under Lieut. E. J. Lake.

Bombay Column.—Brigadier the Hon. H. Dundas (arrived 21st December, 1848).

Artillery :—Major J. S. Leeson.
> 3rd Troop Horse Artillery.
> 2-1st Battn., 4-2nd Battn., 1-4th Battn. and 2-4th Battn. Foot Artillery.

Engineers :—Major W. Scott.
> 1st and 2nd Cos. Sappers & Miners.

Cavalry :—1st Light Cavalry.
> 1st and 2nd Scinde Irregular Horse.

Infantry :—1-60th Rifles, 1st Bombay Europeans.
> 3rd, 4th, 9th and 19th Native Infantry.

Scinde Camel Baggage Corps.

Indus Flotilla :—Capt. F. T. Powell.

Casualties of the Regular Forces :—
> 9 British officers and 201 other ranks killed.
> 55   ,,   ,,   ,, 927   ,,   ,, wounded.

The number of shot and shell fired during the siege was 42,193; but it is uncertain whether this includes the ammunition expended by the Bombay Artillery. At the Siege of Bhurtpore, which lasted 5 weeks (December 1825—January 1826), the expenditure was 61,446 shot and shell.

Troops present at the Battle of Chilianwala, 13th January, 1849 (Lord Gough, C.-in-C.).

Cavalry Division :—Major-General Sir J. Thackwell.
> 1st Brigade :—Brigadier M. White, 3rd Light Dragoons.
> > H.M. 3rd Light Dragoons.
> > 5th and 8th Bengal L. Cavalry.
> 2nd Brigade :—Brigadier A. Pope, 6th Bengal L. Cavalry.
> > H.M. 9th Lancers.
> > 1st and 6th Bengal L. Cavalry.
> > H.M. 14th Light Dragoons (attached).
> 3rd Brigade :—Brigadier J. B. Hearsey (in rear with the baggage).
> > 3rd and 9th Irregular Cavalry.

Bengal Artillery :—Brigadier J. Tennant.
> 2nd Brigade Horse Artillery, 1st, 2nd, 3rd and 4th Troops.
> 3rd Brigade Horse Artillery, 1st and 2nd Troops.
> 1st Battn. Artillery, 1st and 3rd Cos.
> 4th Battn. Artillery, 1st, 2nd and detachment of 4th Cos.
> 7th Battn. Artillery, 3rd Co.

Bengal Engineers :—Major G. B. Tremenheere.
> 4th, 5th, 6th and 7th Cos. Pioneers.

2nd Infantry Division :—Major-General Sir W. R. Gilbert.
    3rd Brigade :—Brigadier C. Godby, 2nd European Regt.
    2nd Bengal European Regt.
    31st and 70th Bengal N. Infantry.
    4th Brigade :—Brigadier A. S. H. Mountain, 29th Foot.
    H.M. 29th Foot.
    30th and 56th Bengal N. Infantry.
3rd Infantry Division :—Brigadier C. Campbell,* 98th Foot.
    5th Brigade :—Brigadier J. Pennycuick, 24th Foot.
    H.M. 24th Foot.
    25th and 45th Bengal N. Infantry.
    7th Brigade :—Brigadier J. Hoggan, 45th Bengal N. Infantry.
    H.M. 61st Foot.
    36th and 46th Bengal N. Infantry.
In reserve :—6th Brigade :—Brigadier N. Penny, 69th Bengal
    N. Infantry.
    15th [20th] and 69th Bengal N. Infantry.
With the Baggage Train :—Brigadier J. B. Hearsey.
    3rd and 9th Irregular Cavalry.
    20th Bengal N. Infantry.
    3 guns 1-1st Battn. Artillery.

Casualties :—
    22 British officers and   580 other ranks killed.
    67   ,,   ,,   ,, 1,584   ,,   ,, wounded.
    104   ,,   ,, missing.
Casualties of H.M. 24th Foot :—
    14 officers and 241 men killed.
    10   ,,   ,, 253   ,, wounded.
12 guns were captured.

Troops present at the Battle of Goojerat, 21st February, 1849 (Lord
    Gough, C.-in-C.).

Cavalry Division :—Sir J. Thackwell.
    1st Brigade :—Brigadier M. White.
    H.M. 3rd Light Dragoons.
    H.M. 9th Lancers.
    8th Bengal L. Cavalry.
    Scinde Irregular Horse.
    2nd Brigade :—Brigadier G. H. Lockwood, 3rd Light Dragoons.
    H.M. 14th Light Dragoons.
    1st Bengal L. Cavalry.
    11th and 14th Irregular Cavalry (each 2 rissalas).
    3rd Brigade :—Brigadier J. B. Hearsey.
    3rd and 9th Irregular Cavalry.

* Afterwards Lord Clyde.

Bengal Artillery :—Brigadier J. Tennant.
Horse Artillery :—1st Brigade, 4th Troop ; 2nd Brigade, 1st, 2nd,
3rd and 4th Troops ; 3rd Brigade, 1st, 2nd and 4th Troops.
Foot Artillery :—1st and 3rd Cos. 1st Battn. ; 2-2nd Battn. ;
3rd and 4th Cos. 3rd Battn. ; 1st, 2nd, and detachment
4th Co. 4th Battn. ; 3rd and 6th Cos. 7th Battn.
Bombay Artillery :—Major J. S. Leeson.
3rd Troop Horse Artillery.
2-1st Battn. (in reserve).

Bengal Engineers :—Brigadier J. Cheape.
2nd and 3rd Cos. Sappers & Miners.
2nd, 3rd, 4th, 5th, 6th and 7th Cos. Pioneers.

Bombay Engineers :—Lieut. W. Kendall.
1st Co. Sappers.

1st Infantry Division :—Major-General W. S. Whish.
1st Brigade :—Brigadier A. Hervey, 52nd N.I.
H.M. 10th Foot.
8th and 52nd Bengal N. Infantry.
2nd Brigade :—Brigadier F. Markham, 32nd Foot.
H.M. 32nd Foot.
51st and 72nd Bengal N. Infantry.

2nd Infantry Division :—Sir W. R. Gilbert.
3rd Brigade :—Brigadier N. Penny.
2nd Bengal European Regt.
31st and 70th Bengal N. Infantry.
4th Brigade :—Brigadier A. S. H. Mountain.
H.M. 29th Foot.
30th and 56th Bengal N. Infantry.

3rd Infantry Division :—Brigadier C. Campbell, 98th Foot.
5th Brigade :—Brigadier A. Carnegy.
H.M. 24th Foot.
25th Bengal N. Infantry (and 45th Bengal N. Infantry
in reserve).
6th Brigade :—Brigadier J. Hoggan.
15th and 20th Bengal N. Infantry (in second line).
(69th Bengal N. Infantry in reserve).
7th Brigade :—Brigadier A. McLeod, 61st Foot.
H.M. 61st Foot.
36th and 46th Bengal N. Infantry.

Bombay Division :—Brigadier Hon. H. Dundas
H.M. 1-60th Rifles.
1st Bombay European Regt.
3rd and 19th Bombay N. Infantry.
Scinde Camel Baggage Corps.

Reserve :—Lieut.-Colonel A. Mercer, 69th Bengal N. Infantry.
          5th and 6th Bengal L. Cavalry.
          2-1st Battn. Bombay Artillery.
          45th and 69th Bengal N. Infantry.
Also present a detachment of the Guides.
Casualties :— 4 British officers and 91 other ranks killed.
             25   ,,   ,,   ,, 681 ,,   ,,   wounded.
56 guns were captured.

*Detached Force near Wazirabad, commanded by Lieut.-Colonel
J. Byrne, 53rd Foot.*

          12th and 13th Irregular Cavalry.
          4 guns 6-7th Battn. Bengal Artillery.
          H.M. 53rd Foot.
          13th Bengal N. Infantry.

On the evening of the 21st February, this detached force had
arrived within a few miles of the right rear of the British Army.
They received the clasp for Goojerat, with the exception of the 13th
Irregular Cavalry, which was probably further to the rear.

Engineer Officers who served in the Punjab Campaign, 1848-9.

Bengal Engineers.

M.G.   Major-General J. Cheape, c.b.   Chief Engineer.
C.G.   Capt. G. B. Tremenheere.
M.G.   Bt. Major R. C. Napier. (Wounded. Chief Engineer at
           Mooltan till December, 1848).
C.G.   Capt. J. Glasfurd.
C.G.   ,,   B. W. Goldie.
C.G.   ,,   H. M. Durand.
M.G.   ,,   W. Abercrombie.
M.G.   ,,   J. R. Western.
M.G.   ,,   H. Siddons.
C.G.   ,,   A. Cunningham.
C.G.   Lieut. C. B. Young.
C.G.   ,,   R. Baird Smith.
C.G.   ,,   A. G. Goodwyn.
 C.   ,,   H. Yule.
C.G.   ,,   T. S. Irwin.
C.G.   ,,   W. E. Morton.
M.G.   .,   J. H. Maxwell.
M.G.   ,,   E. J. Lake. (Political employ).
 M.   ,,   P. Garforth.
 G.   ,,   W. A. Crommelin.
 M.   ,,   G. W. W. Fulton.

M.G. 2nd Lieut. A. Taylor.
M.G.   ,,   A. Fraser. (Adjutant).
M.   ,,   C. S. Paton.
M.G.   ,,   T. G. Glover.
M.   ,,   H. Hyde.
M.   ,,   R. Young.
M.G.   ,,   B. M. Hutchinson. (Mortally wounded at Battle of Goojerat).
M.G.   ,,   F. C. Grindall.
M.G.   ,,   W. W. H. Greathead.
M.G.   ,,   W. S. Oliphant.
M.   ,,   H. W. Gulliver.
M.G.   ,,   C. Pollard. (Wounded).
M.G.   ,,   C. T. Stewart.
M.G.   ,,   F. R. Maunsell.
M.   ,,   A. W. Garnett.
M.G.   ,,   D. C. Home.

Bombay Engineers.

M. Major W. Scott.
M. Lieut. Jno. Hill.
M.G.   ,,   Wm. Kendall.
M.   ,,   H. P. B. Berthon.
M.G.   ,,   J. T. Walker.
M.   ,,   J. W. Playfair.
M.   ,,   J. A. Fuller.

M denotes clasp for the Siege of Mooltan.
C denotes clasp for the Battle of Chilianwala.
G denotes clasp for the Battle of Goojerat.

Medal without Clasp.
Major H. Goodwyn.
Capt. J. R. Oldfield.
Lieut. J. T. Donovan.

These notes have now embraced the period referred to in the introduction, viz. :—1799—1849; but, as the war with China in 1840–2 was carried through almost exclusively by troops from India, a few remarks on the composition of the force and the medal granted for that campaign may not be out of place. The same medal (with the omission of the date) was granted for the subsequent war with China in 1857–60, and notes on this medal necessarily include the clasps granted for that war; and, on account of the fact that the Indian Army was in a transition stage, after the Mutiny, a list of the H.E.I.C. troops employed in China, 1857–60, is given with their designations taken from the medal rolls. In an appendix a similar list is given for the Persian Campaign of 1857; as also certain naval lists which will prove of interest to the collector who specializes.

PLATE X.

EARLY INDIAN CAMPAIGNS AND THE DECORATIONS
AWARDED FOR THEM.

THE PUNJAUB CAMPAIGN. 1848-9.

CHINA WAR, 1840–2.

The occasion of this war was the destruction by the Chinese of British property, valued at £2,500,000, in a violent effort to stop the opium trade. On account of the sea voyage the only Native troops sent from Bengal were volunteers, the bulk of the force being supplied by the Madras Presidency. A good deal of hard fighting took place, before the Chinese sued for peace, which they did just before the British prepared to advance on Nanking. The British possession of Hong Kong dates from this period.

H.E.I.C. Troops that served in the War.

Madras Artillery :—
  C Troop, Horse Brigade.
  B and C Cos. 2nd Battn.
  D Co. 3rd Battn.
  A, B, C, D Cos. China Gun Lascars.
Madras Sappers & Miners :—
  A, B and F Cos.
  Details of C, D and E Cos.
Bombay Artillery :—
  Native detachments serving on board ship.
Infantry :—
  1st Regt. Bengal Volunteers.
  2nd Regt. Bengal Volunteers.
  2nd, 6th, 14th, 37th and 41st Madras N. Infantry.*
  Rifle Company and details of 36th Madras N.I.

List of Officers of the Madras Engineers who served in China, 1840–2.

  Capt. T. T. Pears.
  Lieut. F. C. Cotton.
  Lieut. W. I. Birdwood.
  Lieut. J. C. Shaw.
  Lieut. J. W. Rundall (wounded).
  Lieut. J. Ouchterlony.
  Lieut. J. G. Johnston.
  Lieut. H. W. Hitchins.

For this war a silver medal (described below) was granted, without any clasps ; the suspender being a straight German-silver bar secured to the medal by two concealed pins.

For the war in 1857–60, the same medal (with the date 1842 omitted) was granted, but with a modern curved silver-bar and swivel mounting; and five clasps in all were authorized for the war; a sixth clasp, " China 1842," being granted to those few individuals who were in possession of the medal for 1842.

* The 37th M.N.I. was sent out from India in 1840 ; the 36th M.N.I. in 1841 ; the 2nd Regt. Bengal Volunteers, and 2nd, 6th, 14th, and 41st M.N.I. in 1842.

The 39th M.N.I. garrisoned Hong Kong in 1842, but did not receive the medal.

Medal :—China, 1840–2, 1857–60.

Silver 1·4-in. diameter.
Obverse.—Crowned head of Queen Victoria. Legend " Victoria
    Regina."
Reverse.—A trophy.   Inscription " Armis exposcere pacem."
    " CHINA 1842."
N.B.—" 1842 " is omitted from the medal struck for 1857–60.
Ribbon.—1¼ in. wide.   Red with yellow edges.
Mounting.—(a) 1842.   Straight German-silver bar.
         (b) 1857–60.   Curved silver bar with swivel.
Clasps.—" China 1842."
        " Fatshan 1857" (Navy only).
        " Canton 1857."
        " Taku Forts 1858 " (Navy only).
        " Taku Forts 1860."
        " Pekin 1860."

H.E.I.C. Troops which served in China, 1857–60.

Artillery :—A Co. 5th Battn. Madras Artillery (1860).
            1st Supplemental Co. 5th (Golundaz) Battn. Madras
              Artillery (1860).
            Detachment of Bombay Artillery (and Infantry)
              serving as Marines.
Sappers & Miners :—A and K Cos. Madras Sappers & Miners (1860).
Cavalry :—1st Sikh Cavalry (later 11th Bengal Cavalry) (1860).
          Fane's Horse (later 19th Bengal Cavalry) (1860).
Infantry* :—7th (late 47th) Bengal N.I. (1858–60).
            10th (late 65th) Bengal N.I. (1858–9).
            11th (late 70th) Bengal N.I. (1858–9).
            Detachment 3rd (late 32nd) B.N.I. serving with the
              10th (late 65th) B.N.I. (1858–9).
            New 15th Bengal N.I. (Ludhiana Sikhs) (1860).
             „ 20th Bengal N.I. (late 8th Punjab) (1860).
             „ 22nd Bengal N.I. (late 11th Punjab) (1860).
             „ 23rd Punjab Pioneers (late 15th Punjab) (1860).
             „ 27th Bengal N.I. (late 19th Punjab) (1860).
            Detachment 12th, 29th and 38th Madras N. Infantry
              (1857).
            5th Bombay N. Infantry (1860–2) ; details of 3rd
              Bo.N.I.
            Detachment 21st Bombay N.I. (Marine Battn.)
              serving as Marines.

* The 21st Madras N.I. garrisoned Hong Kong in 1860, but did not
receive the medal.   The 3rd Bombay Infantry were also despatched from
India to China in 1860, but only a few details earned the medal.

From the despatch of the Secretary of State for India to the Governor-General on the subject, and from the 1857–60 medal rolls, it is quite clear that those men who served in *both* wars received in the first instance *only the clasps* to which they were entitled, including the " China 1842 " clasp.

It appears to have been overlooked that the suspender of the " China 1842 " medal was not adapted for the addition of clasps ; but this seems to have been discovered after the issue of the loose clasps had commenced, and medals from the 1857–60 die were then sent out to enable the clasps to be properly fixed. How many of the recipients did this cannot be determined, as the majority were in the Royal Navy, whose medals in 1860 were issued unengraved ; but some undoubtedly had already fixed their clasps to the 1842 medal by altering the original suspender at their own expense.

It may be safely said that very few of the unengraved China medals with the " China 1842 " clasp are *bona-fide* issues. The number of men who earned the " China 1842 " clasp are as follows :—

Royal Navy :—93 in all (including 24 officers).

Army :—6 Europeans and 16 Natives.

Indian Marine :—1 European.

Several of these Natives died before the issue took place, and their medals and clasps were returned to the Horse Guards to be melted.

APPENDIX I.

H.E.I.C. TROOPS WHICH SERVED IN PERSIA, 1857.

Artillery :—Detachments of Bombay Artillery.
Sappers & Miners :—Detachments from Madras and Bombay.
Cavalry :—3rd Bombay Light Cavalry.
　　　　　Detachment Poona Irregular Horse.
　　　　　Scinde Irregular Horse.
　　　　　Aden Irregular Horse.
Infantry :—1st and 2nd Bombay European Regiments.
　　　　　4th, 20th, 23rd and 26th Bombay N.I.
　　　　　2nd Belooch Battalion.
　　　　　Detachments of 2nd, 3rd, 5th, 6th, 8th, 9th, 11th, 15th,
　　　　　　19th, 22nd, 25th, 28th, 29th and Marine Battalion
　　　　　　(21st) Bombay N.I.

APPENDIX II.

LISTS OF VESSELS OF THE INDIAN NAVY EMPLOYED IN VARIOUS CAMPAIGNS.

CHINA, 1840–2.

Bengal Marine.

Enterprise.
Hooghly.
Madagascar.
Nemesis.
Phlegethon.
Pluto.
Proserpine.
Queen.
Tenasserim.

Indian Navy.

Ariadne.
Atalanta.
Auckland.
Medusa.
Sesostris.

CHINA, 1857–60.

Indian Navy.

Auckland.
Berenice.
Coromandel.
Ferooz.
Prince Arthur.
Zenobia.

SCINDE CAMPAIGN, 1843.

The list of vessels employed has been given on page 67. 110 men in all of the " Indus Flotilla " earned the Meeanee medal, and 115 men that for Hyderabad.

PUNJAB CAMPAIGN.

154 Europeans served with the " Indus Flotilla " and earned the medal ; some of them receiving the clasp for " Mooltan " as well.

ARMY OF INDIA MEDAL.

300 medals with the clasp for " Ava " were issued to the Royal Navy, and 46 to European survivors of the Indian Marine. The names of the vessels employed have been given on page 44.

BURMA, 1852–3. (Medal and clasp " Pegu ").

Bengal Marine.

Bhageruttee.
Damoodah.
Enterprize.
Fire Queen.
Indus.
Krishna.
Lord Wm. Bentinck.
Luckea.
Mahanuddy.
Nemesis.
Nerbuddah.
Phlegethon.
Pluto.
Proserpine.
Soane.
Spy.
Sutledge.
Tenasserim.

Indian Navy.

Berenice.
Ferooz.
Medusa.
Moozuffer.
Sesostris.
Zenobia.

PERSIA, 1857. (Medal and clasp " Persia ").

Indian Navy.

Ajdaha.
Assaye.
Assyria.
Berenice.
Clive.
Comet.
Constance.

Euphrates.
Falkland.
Ferooz.
Hugh Lindsay.
Lady Falkland.
Napier.
Nitocris.

Planet.
Punjaub
Semiramis.
Victoria.

INDIAN MUTINY.

300 Europeans of the Indian Marine received the medal. These medals are marked as a rule " Indian Naval Brigade," that being the designation of the force. No clasps were earned by this force.

As regards the Royal Naval Brigade, H.M.S. *Shannon* earned 530 medals, and H.M.S. *Pearl* 232 medals.

In nearly all these campaigns a certain number of Bombay Native Artillerymen received medals, who served on board ship as Marines. The numbers given above do not include these men, as they were only lent by the Army.

FINIS